If you feel alor[...] story and a love worth living for.

    BOB GOFF, bestselling author

I know Sharon Hersh, and I am privileged to be a part of her story. I have witnessed some of the heartache she writes about and the war of desire that she names with raw, stunning, and life-giving truth. This book, like her life, is a song written in the minor key that makes me tremble with the hope that I, too, broken as I am, might be the delight of God. Sharon takes us to the deeper story that always intersects with our worst moments and most mundane days and transforms us as the truest storyteller rewrites what we fear can never be told. *Belonging* will change the trajectory of your story and help you join the stories around you with wisdom and joy.

    DAN B. ALLENDER, PhD, professor of counseling psychology and founding president, The Seattle School of Theology & Psychology; author of *To Be Told*, *The Wounded Heart*, and *Healing the Wounded Heart*

Sharon's book is life-changing. She shares her struggles and brokenness with such daring vulnerability, it makes you feel safe to explore the pages of your own wounded history. I found myself highlighting line after line. So much wisdom and perspective in these pages. I truly believe this book will help so many on the search to understand the center of our "earthquakes" and the healing that is possible when we live our lives with open hands and honesty.

    CINDY MORGAN, singer/songwriter; author

I couldn't stop reading this book. Sharon Hersh is a true sage, and wisdom seeps through each page of costly reflection and bloody experience. I could trust that she had gone before me, cleared the path, and was leading me into the arms of a wildly loving God who was aching for my return home. Buy this book, and be forever marked.

ANDREW J. BAUMAN, author of *Stumbling toward Wholeness*

Belonging is Sharon's most important book yet. We're invited into the ache of the "More" we all long for, not least through Sharon's vulnerable storytelling. In a culture hungry for what is illusive, grasping for what is just out of reach, her story invites us to rest in the Love which is already ours.

CHUCK DeGROAT, professor, therapist, author

Belonging . . . the very title made my heart lurch with longing. Sharon's luscious prose and heart-wrenching transparency freshly illuminated my journey within the narrative of the larger human story God is writing amid the ache and chaos of planet earth. If you, too, are looking to move beyond your secrets, to find transformation through pain, Sharon points us toward a God big enough to sweep us into the community of the beloved. The place where we are finally and ultimately Home.

JEROME DALEY, executive coach and spiritual mentor at Thrive 9 Solutions; author of *Gravitas*

Has the church become an "impostor factory"? Right now, our machine learning and cognitive technology has already surpassed humanity in matters of self-awareness toward relevant, effective responses. For many, this is cause for great concern. But not for those who are brave enough to step out of the narcissism created by unresolved pain and into the realm of authenticity and true community. *Belonging* unravels the mystery of why it's impossible to get close to someone who is always trying to be in control. It reads like a guidebook toward rediscovering the wonder of a six-year-old and courageously invites us to consider what we can learn from Judas about ourselves. If you've ever felt shackled with a burden of pain or loved someone who is trapped in the worst parts of their story, this book—with simplicity and compassion throughout—offers a path toward healing for those who are willing to do the hard and humbling work of facing the inner giants that block our way to freedom.

JUNI FELIX, member of Stanford Behavior Design Lab teaching team; author

(belonging)

Finding
the Way
Back to
One
Another

Sharon A. Hersh

NavPress ®

A NavPress resource published in alliance
with Tyndale House Publishers

NavPress is the publishing ministry of The Navigators, an international Christian organization and leader in personal spiritual development. NavPress is committed to helping people grow spiritually and enjoy lives of meaning and hope through personal and group resources that are biblically rooted, culturally relevant, and highly practical.

For more information, visit NavPress.com.

(dedication)

*for all who
are longing for
Home*

Belonging is a story
that makes you feel at home just by hearing it.
Belonging is like a family where
everything's all right.
Belonging turns a light on in the dark.
It's a love that always cares
and will never leave you.
If you have a heart, it will break.
Belonging heals the broken heart.

Contents

Foreword

BELONGING: FINDING THE WAY BACK TO ONE ANOTHER was a hard book for me to read.

Sharon Hersh is my friend. One of the reasons I like her so much is that she, as much as anybody I know, confesses her sins, is clear about her failures, defines her fears, describes her pain, and reveals who she really is. It's an overused word, but *authentic* is the word that defines Sharon and her story. As I read her book, I found myself saying several times, "I don't believe I would have said that." By the way, that's a positive—rare and refreshing—but it's certainly not the reason this book was hard to read.

It wasn't hard to read because what she wrote isn't true. It's truth on steroids! Not only that. This wasn't a hard book to read because it was difficult to understand or because it was unbiblical or unorthodox. Sharon Hersh writes with a clear, profound, and powerful simplicity, and she always teaches the truth from a solid biblical foundation.

This book was hard to read because Sharon solicits from

her readers, clients, and students the response of "You too?" And that makes self-examination possible (almost mandatory). Frankly, I'm not big into self-examination. I'm doing fine. I'm an old, cynical preacher who just wants to be left alone.

Sharon and Jesus won't leave me alone.

If you want to be left alone, put this book down right now. Don't thank me. I was glad to help.

On the other hand . . .

- if you wince at the division, hatred, and anger within and without the family of God;
- if you grow tired of always trying to prove that you're right, good, and pure;
- if you sometimes think that there has to be a better and more effective way to point others to Christ or even create friendships;
- if you grow tired of the lies you've told yourself and others; and
- if you would like to be free

. . . this book could change your life.

The late Jack Miller (a professor at Westminster Seminary and the founder of Surge, a major world-mission ministry) used to say that the Christian faith can be summed up in two sentences: 1. Cheer up—you're a lot worse than you think you are; and 2. Cheer up—God's grace is a lot bigger than you think it is.

There is a sense in which what is needful is very hard. It feels like dying. But it's also the easiest thing in the world. God really does it all. All it requires is that we take the first step. Then the real God will take the second step. And by the time we get to the third step, we'll know that it was God who took that first step. More important, insofar as we're willing to take the journey, we'll find an exhilarating freedom and an infectious joy. Best of all, God will enable us to love others—and to do it without an agenda.

A number of years ago, my wife and I had dinner with some friends, and Gigi Graham (Billy and Ruth Graham's daughter) was there. As I remember it, the conversation had taken a passionate and rather contentious turn. Gigi said, "I believe that all I'm called to do is to love people. I don't have to change them. That's God's business. I am called to love people no matter their politics, their sexual proclivities, or their belief systems." I said to Gigi that she needed to have some convictions. Gigi replied, "Okay, but I asked my father, and he said I was right." She didn't say it, but her expression shouted it: "So there!"

Just love! What an intriguing idea.

Sharon is going to tell you what she's learned from Jesus. You won't like it, but you'll end up rising and calling her blessed.

Steve Brown, broadcaster, professor, and author of
Talk the Walk: How to Be Right without Being
Insufferable

CHAPTER I

The Way Back

The tale of
someone's life begins
before they are born.
MICHAEL WOOD, *IN SEARCH OF SHAKESPEARE*

I DON'T KNOW HOW MY LIFE became all about me, but it did. Maybe it started when I got straight As on my report card in the third grade. Believing I was enough haunted me later when I got a B in algebra. It energized me when I won "Best Camper" at Rocky Mountain Grace Camp (I'm sure you see the irony). It mocked me when my mom discovered I skipped school for a day in middle school and lied about it. It soothed me when my parents told me I was special. It paralyzed me when I smoked pot with Tommy Ismond during my freshman year of high school (my parents didn't see *that* as so special). My mother's words reverberated in my heart, hot with shame, *"I don't even know if you're a Christian!"* I remember pulling out my dusty Bible for some confirmation, reading Romans 7 in the New Testament and knowing it was written about me: "Yes. I'm full of myself. . . . What I don't understand about myself is that I decide one way, but then I act another, doing things I absolutely despise" (Romans 7:15). My confused sense of self conspired to convince me I needed to become better at hiding my flaws, failures, and mistakes to prove I was good enough, I could make my life work, and I was worthy of love.

My newly resolved strategy of showing off my bright and shiny side while hiding my shadow side worked, but it felt a bit like trying to hold a beach ball underwater twenty-four hours a day, seven days a week. I was exhausted from suppressing part of the truth, protecting my image, and proving I was good enough. And I was lonely. It's impossible to get close to someone who is always trying to be in control.

My story started to shift one Sunday afternoon years after my brief experimentation with marijuana. The secrets of my failed attempts to be enough accumulated faster than the interest on the credit cards I was overindulging on to make my exterior world look good. My marriage broke into a thousand pieces that all the best counselors in the world could not put back together. I started drinking again after being in recovery from alcoholism for years. I was writing a book on relationships and speaking at women's retreats, but I didn't feel like I belonged anywhere. I was heartbroken and ashamed. The weight of me was crushing the life out of me, and I couldn't tell anyone.

At that time, the liquor stores in Colorado were closed on Sundays, and I was desperate for a drink—for an escape from the self that in public acted like I was enough to face the challenges of life and in private knew that I was not. I drove to a local restaurant and sat at the bar, ordering drinks until my mind and heart were numb. I stumbled to my car to make the short drive home, and the most terrible thing I could imagine happened. I glanced in my rearview mirror and saw the flashing lights of the law. It's a blur what happened next—questions I couldn't answer, humiliation stronger than all that booze, handcuffs. I was arrested for driving under the influence. I knew my world would never be the same. I would have to work even harder to erase this hideous blot from my carefully kept record.

I spent a few hours in detox before I was released to a taxicab driver, who took me home. I certainly couldn't call anyone I knew. I fell into my bed, pulled the blankets over my head, and prayed that I would die. How would I ever survive this? Whom could I trust with *this*? Was it possible to save me with the me that had gotten me into this mess in the first place? I remember waking up the next morning and looking at my wrists with a mixture of confusion and terror. Both wrists were marked perfectly in the center with a deep wound. Initially, I wondered what happened . . . and then I remembered the handcuffs.

What kind of a person does such a selfish thing? How could I write and speak about God, his love, his desire for us to love one another—and be such an unlovable person?

We all have stories revealing these kinds of paradoxes, don't we? We are proud, and we hide. We serve, and we feel contempt for others and ourselves. We join, and we isolate. We want God, and we want to *be* god. We bless, and we wound. We are afraid, and we dare greatly. We fall down, and we rise. The paradox within me pushed me further into the dark corners of my life and fueled my determination to try harder, do better, and keep secret anything that might prove my utter inadequacy.

I didn't know then that we don't carry our secrets; they carry us.[1]

Thank God, this secret eventually carried me to a treatment center, where a wise counselor asked me if there was any part of my story I hadn't told anyone. I had already confessed to him about the DUI and couldn't think of any remaining secrets until a few hours later, when the secret I kept even from myself became clear: I hated myself. I felt monstrous and certain that anything beautiful in me had been crushed by the terrible in me. I didn't belong anywhere. All of the whispers I'd tried to silence were true. I wasn't enough. I didn't deserve to be called a Christian. I was unworthy of love. *It was devastatingly all about me.*

The fear of being "found out" in our inadequacies and failures sneaks up on us, much like the police car did in my rearview mirror on that terrible day. It sucker punches us and schools us to cover ourselves with effort, piety, accomplishments, and grandiosity—inevitably resulting in an aching emptiness and sickening shame as we find ourselves sitting in a pile of dust after chasing the wind. This experience of duality, which results in a shaky or false sense of self, is not about the culture, the church, politics, or social media. *It is about us.*

Our narratives—whether they are pinned on Pinterest or spoken as testimonies during small group at church—are filled with words meant to prove ourselves:

- *Everything I need is within me.*
- *I can be the change to make the world great again.*
- *God wants you to be a better you.*
- *Think better and live better.*
- *You can heal your life.*
- *Be your best self, only better.*
- *Visit on Sunday. It's time to soar!*
- *My rights are human rights.*
- *I am enough.*

All this positive self-talk results in stories filled with anxiety, shame, drivenness, pride, guilt, arrogance, entitlement . . . and self:

self-satisfaction self-knowledge
self-importance self-flattery self-acceptance
self-advancement self-preservation
self-help self-righteousness
self-awareness self-destruction self-motivation self-effacement
self-refutation self-deprecation
self-control self-energy self-defense
self-congratulation self-style
self-absorption self-pity self-support
self-will self-love self-improvement
self-fulfillment self-realization
self-security self-taught self-worth
self-consciousness
self-harm
self-image self-justification
self-reliance self-belief self-possession
self-sufficiency self-promotion self-conceit
self-confidence self-improvement
self-expression self-proclamation self-esteem
self-identity self-mastery self-narrative self-hate self-presentation self-advocacy self-analysis self-assurance self-education self-sabotage
self-pleasure
self-delusion
self-indulgence self-praise
self-starting self-seeking

Narcissism: *self-love, self-admiration.*

"Self-love is often rather arrogant than blind; it does not hide our faults from ourselves, but persuades us that they escape the notice of others."—Samuel Johnson[2]

But here is the good news. All of the stories we know and have lived—of success and failure, of *It's all about me* or *Never mind, I don't matter*, of unbelievable selfishness and inexplicable selflessness—mean far more than we know. They are about us and our deep hope to belong to something *More* than us. A confused, false, inflated, or deflated sense of self is not the story God intended for us—but it is the reason we ache for a sense of belonging. It's not that we don't want to belong. We don't know how—

—because we're living by the wrong story.

We need to return to an ancient story that is not tethered to us. This story invites us to know God and the belonging and worthiness he speaks into our lives, enabling us to create a more welcoming world for one another.

When we don't understand *our story*—God's first story about all of us—we waver between entitlement and emptiness, narcissism and nihilism, every man and woman for themselves and "we the people." We become unstable, determined, guarded, grandiose, defensive, and resolve to turn off Twitter because we're afraid of what we might reveal about ourselves or be accused of revealing. Only when we understand *our story* and what it means for our individual stories can we unlearn this muddled sense of self.

In the beautiful book *Between the Dreaming and the Coming True: The Road Home to God*, the author tells the story of a four-year-old girl already longing to find her way back. She is overheard whispering in her newborn brother's ear, *"Baby, tell me what God sounds like. I am starting to forget."*[3] It is the same for us. We can remember what God sounds like only when we return to and recapture the meaning of his first story about us.

Our first story has been lost in translation in a world divided by fear, anger, and alienation. And because of that, we've gotten lost in the plots in our individual stories. When we rediscover the meaning of our first story, we can reorient our individual stories to cast out fear with love, slay anger with grace, and find our way back to one another.

As we bravely face ourselves, the twists and turns in our stories, and the cast of characters around us, we can discover something extraordinary: the innate truth of belonging and worthiness that God writes into our stories. And in discovery, we can start to imagine how to invite others into this greater sense of belonging.

The way back to finding ourselves and one another is not for the faint of heart. It's messy. It's hard work. And it's worth it.

But how do we get there?

When my children were young, our family vehicle was a cherry-red Jeep Grand Cherokee. We referred to that slightly dangerous (no seat belts!) wide-open space in the rear of the vehicle as the "wayback." My kids called dibs on the wayback every time we got in the car, even though they knew they would inevitably be relegated to their neat and tidy (sometimes!), evenly divided, seat-belted places in the second row of the car.

Except when we went on vacations! After a few hours of

sniping, "Mommy, he's breathing on me," or "She touched my elbow," we started to question the wisdom of seat belts. When the sniping turned into all-out pinching and even spitting, we caved: "If you get along, you can ride in the wayback." (I'm not worried that you will judge me, because I know you've been on a few road trips with kids or as a child yourself. Whether with our own children or from our childhood road trips, most of us have experienced some version of this story.) Something magical happened when the rules relaxed, the constraints lifted, and the dividing line disappeared. I actually have fond memories of road trips with my children in the wayback, whispering secrets to each other, putting Band-Aids on their imaginary injuries, becoming allies to survive the long ride home.

It's not so different for us. If we can find the way to unbuckle a few rules we've held on to in relationships, to be released from the constraints of fear and shame, and to erase dividing lines with abandon, the road Home might not be so fraught with perilous potholes and painful skirmishes.

The way back is actually a front-row seat to a tectonic shift, not just on the surface of our lives but in places deep down inside, as we recognize common grace in the beautiful and terrible parts of our lives. In other words, every chapter in our stories, every conversation, and every character is part of the way back to belonging. Common grace becomes transforming grace when we are no longer willing to try to make ourselves with the selves that so often leave us unmade. When we are joined in a deeper story than our individual stories, instead of bickering and squirming away from each other, we can be with one another in compassionate, curious, and creative interactions. We can explore the mystery of being thrown together, knowing we're stuck with one another, so we might as well enjoy the ride.

I invite you to the very edge of your seat to anticipate what could happen in you and others if you engage with the unexpected grace that passionately declares life is not all about our pain, our accomplishments, our rights, our abuse, our power, or our beliefs. *This is about us finding our way. Together.* It is about a supernatural interconnectedness to a deeper Story that infiltrates every nook and cranny of our lives with Light and Love. We can bravely walk into places we never thought we would go, tell the truths we never thought we'd voice, connect with people we never thought we'd spend time with—all while passionately living in a Story tethered to more than us.

My prayer is that somewhere in the process of investigating belonging, we "[raise] the white Gethsemane flag (I surrender, not my will, but yours) . . . anew each day"[4] and discover what God is trying to tell us about *him*. He wants to use every story about us to romance us to his love story and his longing to fill our emptiness with grace, forgiveness, and healing.

Someone once said, "If you want people to know the truth, tell them. If you want people to love the truth, tell them a story." Grace eventually compels us to love the truth because it is telling God's story in us. And when we love the truth, we can't keep from telling that truth to others, because we know—heart and soul—*we belong to each other.*

(into action)

1. Choose a piece of glass with as many different patterns and colors as possible. Find a safe place to take a hammer to that piece of glass, and shatter it into hundreds of little pieces.

   - What did you feel when shattering the glass?
   - Did it feel like a waste?
   - Was it hard to strike the glass so it would break?
   - Did it feel good to break the glass?

2. This is a book about the truth of your story—starting with the ways that you have been harmed and the ways that you have harmed others. All of that brokenness can be difficult to confront or control. It can seem like a waste, a tragedy, or justified vengeance against a world that did not work for you. It can feel humiliating, dangerous, or overwhelming. While reading this book, you might get a chance to see how hard your heart has become, how you learned that you don't matter, why you avoid messy relationships, or why you cling to relationships like they are a savior. Breaking the glass is a way to acknowledge two things:

- **I am willing to tell the truth, no matter the cost.** Living a hidden life behind a plexiglass shield actually costs more than the price of living in the ruins of your brutally honest brokenness. There may be heartache in the ruins, but the reward of telling the truth is abiding in God, because God is truth. It is only living in the truth that breaks the destructive binds that keep us entangled in just ourselves instead of being interconnected to others. Maybe you've felt distant from yourself, others, and God because you have tried to escape the truth.
- **I am willing to wait for God to do something with all those broken pieces.** Are you willing to live in a story that is still being told, accepting that you can't cover, control, or contain the brokenness?

3. Sweep up the dust and broken pieces of glass and put them in a jar. We will come back to this pile of dust and brokenness again and again. Consider this reflection in an Old Testament prophecy: "All go unto one place; all are of the dust, and all turn to dust again" (Ecclesiastes 3:20, KJV).

No one ever told me about the power of these words:
You are dust, and to dust you shall return.
No one ever told me what a gift it would be to return to the ground of my being, to

relinquish the exhausting attempt to fly just a bit above everyone else, to relax my fatigued ego. . . .

On the ground and in the dust there is no façade. No more hiding. Only rest.

And it's where Jesus can find you. Jesus came down, you see. To the dust. In the flesh. And so, you no longer need to prove yourself or protect yourself. There is no ladder to climb, no stairway to the pearly gates, no performance strategy, no purity ritual.

Only surrender. Only rest.

"Come to me, all you who are weary," Jesus says. "Not up there . . . down here!"

No more ladders. No more climbing. Into the dust, where God meets you and renews you.

CHUCK DeGROAT, *FALLING INTO GOODNESS*[5]

(our story of grace)

PART I

[In the beginning] . . . God created human beings; he created them godlike, reflecting God's nature. . . . Then GOD planted a garden in Eden. . . . GOD made all kinds of trees grow from the ground, trees beautiful to look at and good to eat. . . . God commanded the Man, "You can eat from any tree in the garden, except from the Tree-of-Knowledge-of-Good-and-Evil." . . .

The serpent was clever, more clever than any wild animal GOD had made. . . . The serpent told the Woman, ". . . God knows that the moment you eat from that tree, you'll see what's really going on. You'll be just like God. . . ."

[And so the two ate from the tree.] Immediately the two of them did "see what's really going on" [and they were naked and ashamed]. . . . When they heard the sound of GOD strolling in the garden in the evening breeze, the Man and his Wife hid in the trees of the garden, hid from GOD.

GOD called to the Man: "Where are you?"

GENESIS 1–3

CHAPTER 2

The Prelude: Appetites

*The greatest disease in the West today is not TB or
leprosy; it is being unwanted, unloved, and uncared
for. We can cure physical diseases with medicine,
but the only cure for loneliness, despair, and
hopelessness is love. There are many in the world
who are dying for a piece of bread but there are
many more dying for a little love. The poverty in the
West is a different kind of poverty—it is not only a
poverty of loneliness but also of spirituality. There's
a hunger for love, as there is a hunger for God.*

MOTHER TERESA, *A SIMPLE PATH*

WHEN I BOARDED THE LIGHT-RAIL TRAIN to travel into the city,
I was overwhelmed with the sight that greeted me. At 7:00
a.m. on a Saturday morning, the train was already crammed
full of mostly women who seemed to be swimming in a blur
of pink. As my eyes focused, I saw pink hats, pink shirts, pink
signs, and even pink shoes. I immediately knew I somehow
missed an announcement on social media about the dress
code. I pulled my jacket tighter around my gray T-shirt.

And then the train started, and almost as a rehearsed choir,
the train filled with one voice singing a song I did not know:

What I'm trying to say, I'm not sure. . . .
And [this] burning inside me would usually fade.
But it isn't today. . . .
And it is quiet . . .
Like I've sailed into the eye of the storm.[1]

There was a moment of quiet after the song, and then it began again—louder the next time. As I was caught up in the melody of voices and the lyrics of resolve, I knew why the train was packed full on an early Saturday morning. I felt the power of belonging to something more than myself.

I didn't know it then, but later the people on that train would join over 150,000 others in my city—mostly women in their pink apparel, gathering to participate in a collective march making a statement of purpose and passion, a tradition that is older than America. The Women's March of January 21, 2017, became a phenomenon greater than its social-media roots or any political party or cultural agenda. As people later debated why they marched or argued that this worldwide march of millions of people was questionable, no one could argue that something happened on that Saturday morning that felt dangerous—

—like it could take on a life of its own.

Perhaps that's how citizen-soldiers or their families felt when they joined the revolution to fight for an independent country with its own laws and rights. I think that's how people might have felt as they linked arms many years later under the banner of civil rights. They sang songs then, too: "We shall overcome, some day."[2]

A week following the Women's March, hundreds of thousands gathered to passionately proclaim a fight for life and the rights of the unborn. As I stood in the midst of a second gathering mob of pink, I remembered what Philip Yancey once wrote (quoting author and ethicist Lewis Smedes) after attending one of the first gay rights marches with a friend who had recently announced he was gay: "The first and often the only person to be healed by forgiveness is the person who does the forgiveness."[3] I prayed that these two protests of women in pink might begin a process of forgiveness and healing in our deeply divided country.

That hasn't happened. Yet.

I am not writing about these modern-day marches to promote a political agenda, but rather to affirm that there is something in those events—these passionate protests for the protection of human rights—that is a sign of what we were made for. All of the signs carried by people who share a cause point to a reality we have seen in many places and at many times in history. As psychiatrist Oliver Sacks explains,

> To live on a day-to-day basis is insufficient for
> human beings; we need to transcend, transport,
> escape; we need meaning, understanding, and
> explanation; we need to see over-all patterns in our

lives. We need hope, the sense of a future. And we need freedom.[4]

Whether marching or joining with others to critique the march, we reveal in mass numbers our human appetite for *More*—to belong to something or someone besides ourselves.

> **Transcendence:** *a state of being or existence above or beyond the material.*
>
> *"If [we] have trouble letting go of material needs, then [we] will have a difficult time achieving transcendence."*[5]

The longing for transcendence may pull us to political activism, a fantasy-football league, or the heart-pounding, palm-sweating world of Internet dating. Even if you don't join social causes or you don't eat too much, drink too much, or spend too much, I suspect you've felt this craving for *More*. Maybe it's in the moments right before you drift off to sleep, or when you're driving home from work and your mind starts to wander, or when you're loading the dishwasher after dinner and you feel heartache for a moment—and you wonder, *Is this is all there is to life, or is there* More? *And if there is more, how can you get it? Where can you find it, or who can offer you even a taste of belonging to something more than yourself (even if it means going on a first date with a stranger you swiped toward on Bumble!)?*

I know this human reality because I am aware of my

own heart. I'm prone to wander into daily, dull, or even dangerous places, looking for fulfillment, relief from stress and pain, or a sense of control in an out-of-control world—and I end up discovering that not only can I not complete myself, soothe myself, or conquer myself with myself, I often only intensify that longing for *More*. I can't find the code to unlock that vault to a place that feels like Home—a place where I belong.

In the midst of the ache and our strategies to satisfy that ache, we all too often turn against each other. In his brilliant essay "The Politics of the Brokenhearted," Parker Palmer writes of the "heart broken by unbearable tension into a thousand shards—shards that sometimes become shrapnel aimed at the source of our pain." He goes on to describe how the anguish of not belonging to more than ourselves can often become a weapon to cause further alienation: "Here the broken heart is an unresolved wound that we too often inflict on others."[6] Our appetite for *More* becomes a clenched fist against God and others instead of "a heart 'broken open' into largeness of life, into greater capacity to hold one's own and the world's pain and joy."[7]

Desire has been a confusing reality we have used against one another from the beginning. Perhaps the first story of desire gone awry has a larger purpose: to inform all our stories of desperately seeking to have enough, do enough, and be enough only to end up wanting. Could it be that the prelude to our story is designed to make us ache for more of God and one another?

21

From the Beginning

God's first story about all of us is about a man and a woman whose lives were quickly gobbled up by their desires and demands, faith and doubt, defiance and shame, and a commitment to be gods. This story in the Old Testament book of Genesis is important because it is God's story about the genesis of us. His-story is our story. *It is about us.*

As the plot of God's first story about us unfolds, we learn the story will take place in a Garden where everything works. It's Paradise! God plants Adam and Eve in the most luxurious resort community imaginable—they have it all. But it's not enough. They are restless and feel out of sorts. It's like being at the Four Seasons in Maui and wishing you'd packed different clothes and traveled with different people. And you're hungry!

The prelude to our story reveals that we were *created* with an appetite for *More*. We were created to be joined to more than Paradise-perfect spouses (Adam and Eve hadn't even thought about, much less fought about, the right way to squeeze the toothpaste yet) and an all-inclusive buffet. Our longing for *More* was there before God asked Adam and Eve not to eat of the fruit of the Tree-of-Knowledge-of-Good-and-Evil.

It's almost like God said, "Even though I have planted you in Paradise, I know that won't be enough for you, and to prove it, I'm asking you not to eat from just one tree— the Tree-of-Knowledge-of-Good-and-Evil." Have you ever pondered what was so dangerous about the fruit of this particular tree that God made it the only thing off-limits?

Consider for a moment that the first couple's appetite for the forbidden fruit of knowing everything about good and evil was present *before* they disobeyed God. They had everything, and it still wasn't enough. God knew that's how the story would go because *he* created Adam and Eve with insatiable appetites. Does that mean God was setting us up from the beginning? And if so, for what? The story of creation, after all, ends like this: "God saw all that he had made, and it was very good" (Genesis 1:31, NIV).

Everything God made was very good—even, and maybe especially, the man and the woman with an appetite for *More*. God was not caught off guard by Adam and Eve's decision to listen to the snake and eat the forbidden fruit. He knew they would try to write themselves out of the story he was telling because they thought they could have *More by knowing everything about how to make life work*—even in Paradise. Adam and Eve thought if they could know enough and have enough control to write their own stories, to be their own storytellers, just maybe they could control or get rid of that hunger for *More* and feel like they belonged.

The Genesis story reveals that our human appetite for *More* can be dangerous. We can start looking for *More* in all the wrong places and in all the wrong ways. Our appetite for *More* often translates into an ugly fight for rights, an empty escape into numbness from the tension with drugs or alcohol, an accumulation of false power in expensive possessions or prominent positions, or even a faith in our abilities to save ourselves by being better.

In her book *Appetites*, Carolyn Knapp writes, "The great preoccupation with things like food . . . is less of a genuine focus on hunger . . . than it is a monumental distraction from hunger."[8] What are we really hungry for? We try to satiate our desire for *More* in as many ways as there are personalities—through control, relationships, accomplishments, activism, pleasure, knowledge, health, and even spirituality. We seek a holiday from the dailiness of life or immediate gratification in the disappointment of life. Our appetites compel us to want more than a taste of beauty, power, and goodness. We long to rise up to own the beauty, power, and goodness of the world we live in, hoping we will not feel so out of control, out of place, out of understanding.

Adam and Eve allowed the crafty serpent to convince them they could own beauty, power, and goodness if they could just know enough, be good enough, avoid evil enough, and be in control enough. Adam and Eve did not know that the serpent only told them half of the truth: They could have more control over their story—but in gaining control, their story became less, not more. Scripture says they could see what was going on after they ate the fruit, and they saw that they were naked—and were ashamed. With sudden clarity, they knew they could not satisfy themselves with themselves. They didn't feel like they belonged more. They felt like they belonged less.

Adam and Eve's story—our genesis story—suggests that

there are different ways to deal with our desire for *More*. We can try to willfully take *More* for our own purposes, like the first man and woman, or we can receive *More* as a gift. Perhaps their impoverished experience of *More* is a necessary part of the parable to send us in a different direction—away from ourselves and back toward God and each other.

It's not that God doesn't want to give us *More*—it's that he knows we can only claim a shadow version on our own. For me, that shadow version was my struggle with alcohol dependence. It has been my forbidden fruit. I initially thought it would bring more peace, camaraderie, and freedom. It eventually brought me not only to the back seat of a police car but to more anxiety, loneliness, and bondage.

For a time, the counterfeit version of *More* still offered me a sense of control and a way of knowing how to manage the loneliness in my life, but that knowledge separated me from God and from others. I couldn't be my true self, altered by more booze, and others couldn't be their true selves with me—altered by more confusion, fear, and anger over my behavior. My experience with alcoholism is a good example of how knowledge, or a means to control life, diminishes us to shadows of ourselves—just oversimplified facts. I was an alcoholic, a criminal, a woman numb to those around me. Others were obstacles to my getting more booze, judgmental, fearful, and hurting. It pains me to write those descriptors of myself, friends, and family members, but that is what our attempt to control our longings does. It reduces us to less, not more.

So how do we fill this ache for *More*? We can know things greater than ourselves through wonder and worship— relationship with God. Years ago, when my son was six, he stayed up to watch his first Fourth of July fireworks display. We sat on our deck, and as if by magic, the spectacular sparkling light show appeared right above our heads. Graham looked at me, with tears in his eyes, and whispered, "Mom, look what God is doing just for us." He tasted God apart from any facts or theological knowledge. He feasted on God freely. Every morsel was a gift.

We can also experience more from others—heart and soul—but only if they choose to reveal more and we receive it by grace. One of my most beloved clients had schizophrenia. Kyle often came to counseling disoriented about time and daily events. Prior to one of his appointments, I received an email from a friend that cut me to the core. As Kyle arrived, I tried to set aside my friend's awful words and put on my professional self. Kyle sat down and made his usual surveillance of my office, and then he looked right at me. With clear eyes, he asked, "Are you okay?" Caught off guard, I answered honestly: "I just got a really hurtful email from a friend." Without a pause, Kyle softly replied, "Love will have the final word. It always does." Kyle didn't understand his disease or know any facts about my relationship heartache, but *More* showed up in my office that day simply because Kyle gave to me freely and I could receive, undefended by pride or any sense of control.

Is it possible, then, to make choices that allow us to be

more fully known and to truly know the hearts of others? To experience more of this gift of belonging?

The answer to this question is more important than ever. "Health insurer Cigna took a nationwide survey of 20,000 adults and found that 54% of respondents said they feel like no one actually knows them well. . . . Additionally, 56% of people said the people they surround themselves [with] 'are not necessarily with them,' and approximately 40% said they 'lack companionship,' their 'relationships aren't meaningful,' and that they feel 'isolated from others.'"[9] No wonder we have become one nation, divided, with anger and pain for all.

The irony in God's first story about us uncovers that the more we try to conquer knowledge, the less we may know. The more we try to make life work, the less it really works—in our hearts and souls, where we experience *More*. The more we try to belong, the less we receive the gifts of belonging. As a result of believing the snake's lie, Adam and Eve took fruit from the Tree-of-Knowledge and they lost knowing—deeply knowing themselves and God. They took what they believed they had a right to take and lost wholehearted relationship with each other and communion with God.

We experience this first story in our individual stories. When was the last time you felt fully yourself, honest and unhindered, alongside others who were able to be fully themselves? In the midst of all our knowledge and attempts to makes life work, we rarely experience the wonder of a six-year-old or the wisdom of an unguarded mind. We don't need to spend much time on Twitter to see the lengths we go in order to keep one another at arm's length, not trusting other people's motives, words, or perspectives. We have reaped the harvest of the fruit of the Tree-of-Knowledge-of-Good-and-Evil. All the knowledge in the world will not lead us to the gifts of trusting each other for real relationship, to the kind of life-giving connection that challenges, encourages, and leads us to God.

We're still hungry.

When the Story Doesn't Seem Good

When my daughter turned thirteen, she was filled with the normal angst of adolescence. One afternoon her distress turned to confusion, and I found her sobbing in her bedroom. When I asked what was wrong, she said, "Mom, why do I want so much? I don't want to leave middle school. I'm afraid I'll lose all my friends when we change schools. And will I ever have a boyfriend?" She continued in the stream-of-consciousness dialogue that seems logical in the mind of a teenage girl, "All of my other friends have had boyfriends, and I've never even held hands with a boy. I probably will never be kissed. Oh, Mom, what is wrong with me?"

If I'm honest, I wanted to hug her tightly and soothe away her questions with some practicality: "You're right, Kristin. You shouldn't want so much. In fact, if you don't want so much, you will be less likely to be disappointed." Instead, I told her the truth—as dangerous as it can be: "All that you are longing for right now is not a sign of something wrong with you, but something more profoundly right with you than you can possibly imagine." I didn't know it then, but I was paraphrasing the perilous wisdom of C. S. Lewis, who believed that our problem with desire isn't that we want too much, but that we want too little.[10]

The story of Adam and Eve and the longing for *More* that took them to heart-wrenching places—where they actually experienced less—is one I've known personally. When my marriage fell apart, I worked hard to distract myself from the pain with work, hobbies, and addictions. I believed if I could stay away from the ache, I would be better off. Then I read Parker Palmer's essay, written shortly after my marriage ended. He wrote of a grief of his own, saying, "I must allow myself to go to the center of my pain and stay there until I have felt it as fully as I can."[11] That sounded insane to me, but my strategy of pragmatic detachment was not working. For days, I let the pain wash over me. I wept until there were no more tears. I understood Palmer's words: "Somehow, I had turned a corner toward healing, toward a place where my heartbreak was more likely to serve life."[12] In the wake of honestly acknowledging my grief over loss and my holy hunger for relationship, I returned to church, leaned into friendships, and began to rest from the frantic pace of running from the pain.

Author and storyteller Michael Meade once wrote, "A story is a store or a storehouse. Things are actually stored in the story."[13] What is stored in this genesis story of desire? Sometimes it seems, just as in my daughter's adolescent story, that good appetites only reveal hunger pains. Other times, like when I was grieving my divorce, acknowledging hunger pains reveals good appetites.

Our favorite stories—from childhood fairy tales to modern-day blockbuster movies—are filled with the tension of getting a taste of something good only to be left with the heart-wrenching need for *More*. A sermon my pastor preached about these stories got me to thinking about our love-hate relationship with our appetites, and how the stories I love, just like the stories I have walked through, unearth something deeper.[14]

Themes: *The themes in our stories tell who we are and give our stories meaning. We are a mosaic made up of meaning we can never get to until we start to understand the themes of our stories.*

- One of the first fairy tales I remember reading is the one of Snow White, who already was the most beautiful, most desirable, and most favored woman in the kingdom. Still, she was tricked by her jealous, evil stepmother into taking a bite of irresistible fruit. She fell lifeless to the floor after one bite. Why did she have to take that fateful bite when she already had everything, only to lose her life in her appetite for *More*?

- I cried with my children when we watched *The Lion King* as the young Simba exuberantly pursued more—more power, more understanding, and more ways to feel in control—and then fell into a bottomless pit of sorrow when his father, the lion king, died. I wanted to turn off the story when another lion, Scar, who desperately wanted to be king, seized the moment of inexplicable pain-filled longing and snarled, "If it weren't for you, he'd still be alive! . . . Run away, Simba! Run. Run away, and never return!" How could love, longing, and companions be so cruel?

• I will admit I watch reality television and have even shed a few tears as I've watched the bachelorettes compete for the prized rose from *The Bachelor*. It's painful to watch the sometimes embarrassing or desperate antics of the women who want *More*—more time, more attention, more love—and still are not chosen. My now-adult daughter echoed my sentiments about this show when she lamented to me, "I can't watch it. Why would people even agree to be on a show when they are pretty much guaranteed to be rejected?"

• My son and I loved watching all the Star Wars stories. My heart swelled with pride as the noble Obi-Wan Kenobi—Jedi master—agreed to teach the young Anakin Skywalker, until the story turned. Obi-Wan found himself in a battle with Anakin, now grown and twisted into Darth Vader, who contemptuously growled as he fought for *More*, "The circle is now complete. When I left you, I was but the learner. Now *I* am the master." To my shock and sorrow, Vader appeared to slash the old teacher with his saber, cutting him in half. The story quickly turned from one of adventure to one of horror.

- Similarly, in The Lord of the Rings, my hopes for the brave fellowship were dashed when the wise Gandalf was swallowed up in an overwhelming battle with evil. As the Balrog advances, Gandalf is whipped, staggers, reaches for a handhold—and then, before he slides into the abyss, he cries to all those watching in horror, "Fly, you fools." His companions are paralyzed in the dark, staring into the pit where Gandalf has fallen. The movie poignantly reveals the potentially treacherous risk of pursuing good only to see everything go bad.

Could it be that stored in these stories is *our story*? Is God still telling our story even when desire takes a turn toward loss, failure, humiliation, and even death? Is it possible, even in bad stories, that the story God is telling is still good, even very good? That's hard to believe, isn't it? A story that starts with a relentless pursuit of *More* that never seems to be satisfied and sets us up to make mistakes, forcing us to get back up and try again, only to inevitably leave us with more longing, greater pain, and a deeper sense that there will never be enough—well, that seems like a bad story.

We feel those hunger pains in our real-life stories too.

To believe those stories are good—especially when we only see a page or two of the story at a time—is especially hard. Think about the painful chapters in your story—as a teenager, spouse, parent, coworker, child. Perhaps there's a chapter of love lost to infidelity; a chapter of dreams shattered in bankruptcy; a chapter of youth swallowed up by addiction; or a chapter of faith decimated by abuse.

Our own unsatisfactory chapters in our stories make us quick to judge others by one page in their stories and conclude in contempt or despair, "This is not a good story!" Or we take one page of our own story and judge the Storyteller with contempt or despair: "You are not writing a very good story!" It's perhaps hardest to believe that, even when we or someone we know listens to the serpent's ideas about desire and makes a disastrous decision, God is still writing a good story.

> **Contempt:** *An attempt to gain a sense of control in a world where there is more tragedy than we can comprehend. Contempt expressed toward others or ourselves is a conscious or subconscious demand that someone pay for the pain in this world.*

But I think God is keeping us on the edge of our seats. We feel the allure of desire as we read fairy tales and watch stories of romance and adventure. We experience the roller-coaster reality that the greater the story, the greater the potential for pain. And we lean into the longing for *More.*

From Here to Eternity

If God is the Storyteller, then from our first story and every story after, we are all part of a *good* story God is telling. That would mean Adam and Eve's bite from the forbidden fruit is not the most important part of the story. Part of the good news in your story is that your biggest mistake or the failure of someone you love is not the most important part of *your* story. Maybe *you* are not the most important part of your story. Our choices, behaviors, mistakes, and protests are really stories within *the story*—the story that God begins in Genesis, continues throughout the rest of the Bible, and finishes in the one who is the Way, the Truth, and Life itself.

Perhaps the prelude to our story—our appetite for *More*—is not even the most important part of the story. What is important, though, is that our God-created appetites provoke a few questions we will consider in the rest of this book:

- Why did God design us with something so innate that it might compel us to write him out of the story?
- Why keep reading a story by an author who keeps us wanting *More*?
- What or who has the most power in this story—the appetite, the characters, or God?
- Does the ensuing carnage from our attempts to conquer *More* overpower God's love?
- Is it possible for someone to turn God into merely a fact in the story, so it is no longer His-story?

(Especially someone who believes in and makes different choices than we would in search of *More?*)

- What is the most important page in your story—is it one about your goodness or your badness?

And what about the pages in other people's stories? That question reminds me again of being in that sea of pink and seeing signs that made me uncomfortable, that offended me, and that I just didn't understand. There were moments I wanted to get off the train. I knew the signs were symbols of wanting to belong to something *More*, but they were asking for it in ways that were painful to others. It felt like watching all those scenes in the movies when we just want to stop watching . . . but we can't. We have to see the way *More* takes us.

We were made for it.

Maybe understanding that we all long for *More* can encourage us to stop judging ourselves or other people for where they are in their stories. When we judge ourselves or others, it's like ripping one page out of the story and throwing the rest of it in the trash. We can't even begin to understand all the factors that led to the actions on one particular page. Maybe our longing for *More* can take us toward one another instead of away from one another.

Most importantly, perhaps, acknowledging our shared longing for *More* can keep us from judging God. We don't know why he has included a page in the story for one person and not another. We haven't read all the pages in his story yet either. But before we can understand the big picture of his story, we have to find a way to hold the tension in this prelude—our God-given appetites that have, from God's first story about us, gotten us into trouble or pain-filled places. Can we rest in God's pronouncement that this is a good story—even though he knew about the snake, he planted the tree with the forbidden fruit in the Garden, he knew Adam and Eve would not be able to resist, and he knew the result of their choice would be loss? Can we believe, even, that this is a *very* good story?

Perhaps we can better live with the tension of the prelude if we remember our human experience with stories: We actually get more interested in the plot if we don't know exactly where the story is going. We're more curious about the meaning of a story if the author doesn't tell us the meaning up front.

- We read *Snow White* because we're holding our breath in the hope that a prince with a magical kiss might be right around the corner.

- We watch *The Lion King*, waiting for Simba to emerge from painful exile and take his rightful place as the lion king.

- The possibility of a real love story keeps us watching *The Bachelor* and *The Bachelorette* for yet another round of roses.

- When I saw the first Star Wars movie in the theater as a young adult, I just couldn't believe that Obi-Wan

Kenobi was really dead. It took me a while to wonder who might be hiding under the villainous Darth Vader's mask—and to look for the redemption that might be coming.

- By the time the Lord of the Rings books were being made into movies, I had a sense of how these kinds of stories go. When Gandalf was cast into the abyss, I didn't let go of hope. I knew he would rise again.

The prelude to our story is important. It compels us to keep reading, to not give up on the story or the Storyteller, on a person, or on ourselves—even if the story is filled with snakes, painful longings, bad decisions, and even death. As the brilliant storyteller J. R. R. Tolkien demonstrated in his stories swelling with tides of impending doom, you can't keep the gospel out of stories. An unlikely hero, an unexpected ally, a startling rescue is coming in the next wave. We can't keep the Good News out of stories, because even bad stories nurture a longing for the good Story.

Thinking about God's first story in this way—and thinking about your story or the stories of others in this way—might be a bit unsettling because everything is not yet resolved. It might be hard to identify anything good in the bad. Just thinking about our longing for *More* can remind us of painful stories from the playgrounds of our childhoods when we were picked last for the kickball team, or humiliating stories from high school when we didn't have a date for the homecoming dance. Thinking about appetites might make us think about parents or spouses whose appetites were out of control in addiction or anger.

When we don't know what to do with our longing for *More*, our failed attempts to satisfy those longings, or God's intention in creating us with such insatiable appetites in the first place, it's easier to judge the stories than to trust the Storyteller. We end up coming to conclusions that unravel our connection to God and each other, that push us further and further from belonging:

- What are all those protesters screaming about? They don't need more rights.
- She may be pretty, but she doesn't have much to say.
- He killed the hopes and dreams of a lot of people with some stupid tweets.
- He's a beast, and I won't trust him.
- No one ever picks me. I will never belong.
- It's foolish to trust anyone.
- The self-absorbed win in the end.

Stories, and especially God's stories, feel dangerous. They feel like the dark, unresolved pieces of our own stories. Eve ate forbidden fruit; Adam remained silent; Cain killed his brother; Rahab was a prostitute; Moses couldn't control his temper; David should never have been made king; Ruth was an unwelcome immigrant; Elijah was suicidal; the prophets were embarrassing; Jesus was born to a poor, unwed mother;

the disciples were uneducated and fueled by jealousy, doubt, and betrayal; Paul was a murderer—and that's not even half of the stories in the Bible.

But in each of these stories, there were pages still to be written and to be read. And in our own stories, the reason things feel unresolved is because we are living in the middle of what God is writing. He is writing to lead us toward what we long for most deeply: to be known, to be loved, and to be able to freely love others as we've been loved. So don't throw away anyone's story—especially your story. Search for the truths in your story relentlessly, and then guard them carefully. Keep reading. Understanding our deepest longings almost always comes at great cost. We feel hungry. We try to satisfy our hunger in the wrong ways and the wrong places. We feel exposed and ashamed. We try to hide from ourselves, others, and God. But that is not the end of the story. It is just the prelude to a much larger story about a battle long, long ago, a battle that was not against people but *for* people. *A battle that was about us.*

(into action)

1. Pick a favorite story from childhood—The Chronicles of Narnia, *The Little Red Hen*, "Beauty and the Beast," *Old Yeller, Charlotte's Web, Harry Potter and the Sorcerer's Stone*, A Series of Unfortunate Events, etc. Look for the place in the story when you feel the

longing for *More*—in the tension of waiting, failure, misunderstanding, or heartache. Imagine throwing away the book at that point. What would you miss if you didn't read the rest of the story?

2. Look at your jar of dust and broken pieces. What stories of your own come to mind when you wanted to quit on yourself, others, or God? What would you have missed if you'd been able to quit the story? Are people you love at heart-wrenching points in their stories? What do you believe about them as a result of the page they are on in their story?

3. Select a few pieces of glass to represent painful places in your story or the stories of others you care about. Put these pieces of glass somewhere you can see them throughout the day. When they catch your eye, consider the idea that those shattered places in the story are gifts. Yes, they may be gifts that cut your hands and make them bleed, but they are gifts to make you long for *More* and make you ready for the one whose name is *More*.

If it's hard to raise the white flag then it's harder to
    believe
That surrendering is worth the sacrifice
Because the very thing I always feared
would be the death of me
Was a way to come alive

It hurts to be so broken
But it's bearable somehow
As the grounds to prove I'm worthy disappear
I've always heard you loved me
And I think I know it now
It's a reason why you brought me here
Love's a reason why you brought me here

ANDY GULLAHORN, "WHY YOU BROUGHT ME HERE"[15]

CHAPTER 3

The Cast of Characters

To become aware of the possibility of the search is to be onto something. Not to be onto something is to be in despair.

WALKER PERCY, *THE MOVIEGOER*

HE WAS ONTO SOMETHING. After months of feeling ashamed and depressed, Tyler started to feel something that he had not felt in a long time: hope. Tyler came to see me for counseling when he was a senior in high school. I could tell immediately he was highly intelligent and highly sensitive—a potentially terrible mix for an adolescent boy trying to navigate the world of high school. He didn't like sports and wasn't very athletic. He was certain about the formulas in physics but started doubting God years earlier, when the formulas that he'd heard in church didn't work. He'd heard that if he loved God, tried to do the right things, and made his family proud, he would be happy. That equation did not come true for

Tyler. He didn't have a lot of friends who understood him. He was lonely. He didn't know how to talk about his internal world with his parents, and they didn't know how to talk to him. He was stuck in a mire of conflicting emotions.

When Tyler was eight years old, he had a best friend. He liked math and movies, just like Tyler. He got straight As and had never played a team sport for longer than one season, just like Tyler. His family was a conservative suburban family who scurried to get everyone off to church on Sunday morning but never talked about any of what they'd heard on Monday or any other day of the week, just like Tyler's family. Tyler and his best friend spent almost every weekend together—often spending the night at each other's homes.

When they were both twelve, the safety of their long-term friendship, combined with a normal developmental curiosity about their bodies and themselves, cajoled Tyler and his friend to explore their questions about sex with each other. The result was they were embarrassed and intrigued, afraid and excited, and their exploration quickly became a ritual in their time together. Tyler knew his parents would be shocked or even worse, and he wasn't sure what this relationship was saying about him, about his sexuality, or about God.

When Tyler started high school, his friend moved to another city, and their time together came to a halt, leaving Tyler lonelier than he thought possible. He hated himself for wanting something he thought he shouldn't want. He resented his parents for creating an environment where they never really talked about anything more than his homework or the headlines from the nightly news because they were busy creating a life that looked good and didn't have time for anything that might be messy. Tyler wanted his peers to like him but was terrified for them to really know him, because he had heard their judgments about people who weren't like them. And Tyler gave up on God. He was certain God had given up on him during one of those middle-of-the-night trysts that felt so dangerous and also felt more like belonging than anything else in Tyler's world.

When Tyler came to see me, he had tried out for the school play—*The Passion of the Christ*—and had been cast in one of the lead roles. Tyler was chosen for the character Judas—the one who betrayed Jesus, sold his whereabouts to the authorities for a pile of silver, felt disgusted with himself, didn't trust any of his friends, and eventually went out and hanged himself. As a mother, I understood why Tyler's mom was concerned about his passion for this dark character (which is why she sent him to counseling). Tyler did not empathize with his mom. "I really think I'm onto something," he told me. "I understand Judas. His character is making me rethink what I believe about me and about God. In fact, I think I believe this story about Jesus more than ever!"

Can you believe that? God used a lonely boy's questions about sex—and a story about a scandalous liar who eventually died by suicide—as an entry to Tyler's heart? Suddenly Tyler recognized his story was contained within *this* story. He understood the despair of Judas, but he also became intrigued by the other characters in the story—Peter, who also betrayed but found comfort in the one whom he betrayed; Thomas, who also doubted but kept asking questions of the one he doubted; and Jesus, the one who was betrayed but shared bread and wine with Judas, knowing he had already double-crossed him. Jesus also knew that he himself would soon hang on a cross for the sins of the world, where he would utter a special prayer for those who thought they were the worst sinners: "Father, forgive them, for they do not know what they are doing" (Luke 23:34, NIV). Tyler was more intrigued by Jesus as a result of the story of Judas because he no longer felt as alone or as distant from this story of God: It was, after all, filled with people and motives and emotions that felt very similar to his own.

The cast of characters in God's larger story helps us understand ourselves in profound ways because all our stories have a cast of characters—victims, perpetrators, bystanders, and heroes. Even though these characters take up a lot of space in our stories, more often than not, the most important character in our stories is us. We play the part of the victim, perpetrator, and bystander, and then we hope we can be the hero who rescues us from ourselves—though that often leaves us feeling separate from others.

If we don't confront the characters in our stories and understand their roles, we will be hidden from our true selves. We come into this world whole, expressing all sorts of needs without constraint. But as we grow older, we quickly learn that parts of ourselves are embarrassing, unacceptable, and rejected by others—and we learn to hide these parts of ourselves. The gap between our hidden self and public self creates a chasm where woundedness and confusion grow, making us more determined to find something to numb, cover, or distract us from the pain of feeling like we don't belong. So we find ourselves further and further from one another.

When we don't understand our longings or the confusing characters in our lives, we often experience this coming apart. We believe the resulting sense of nakedness, humiliation, shame, and distance from God is where it all goes wrong. But the characters who matter in our stories reveal a lot about what matters most to us and are often signposts to some of the tricky or treacherous turns we take in our lives. These characters can either point us to a deeper story that contains our stories or justify our staying stuck in ourselves and our self-destructive choices.

Which character takes up the most space in your story? Is it a friend who betrayed you, parents who doubted you, a spouse or child suffering from mental illness, fellow church-goers who don't really know you . . . or is it you? The answer to this question will reveal how you see yourself—a victim, a perpetrator, a failure, a cynic, or someone alone against the world.

If we don't really believe in a story that is deeper than our own stories, we'll be committed to blaming the characters in our stories. We will construct a narrative filled with our justifications, our knowledge of right, and our good deeds. When we live in a narrative constructed out of the fear of coming face-to-face with the whole truth of our stories and with the Storyteller, we separate from ourselves, one another, and God—and that's actually bondage and death. Blaming the cast of characters is a way to be numb to life—and to love.

> **Blameshifting:** *placing the entire responsibility for our unpleasant actions, consequences, or feelings on another person while insisting others agree with our perspective of blame. By blameshifting, we can block vulnerability and intimacy.*

But the cast of characters in our lives—if we're ready to truly understand who they are—can also point the way to life. We cannot understand our salvation story without a cast of characters that includes the impoverished, the failures, the outcast, the naked, the ashamed, and the lost—all desperate to find a home. The impoverished ask us to consider the one who became poor that we might be made rich (2 Corinthians 8:9); the failures and outcasts humble us to bow before the one who became a curse so we might be blameless (Galatians 3:13); the naked compel us to consider the one who promises to be our covering (Isaiah 4:6); the ashamed draw us to that beautiful, terrible moment when the Fatherless Son was nailed to the tree by the Sonless Father, who was forced to look away so we could be called the children of God (Matthew 27:46; 1 John 3:1). The lost and wandering tell the story of the homeless God-With-Us who did not even have a place to lay his head, and yet was even then dreaming of the Home he is preparing for us (Luke 9:58; John 14:3).

Without desire gone awry, nakedness, humiliation, shame, and a cast of imperfect characters, we would have no salvation story. Understanding the brokenness in our story—of ourselves and all the other people in our story—is essential for us to become whole, and it is necessary for us to begin to heal the wounds in our divided world.

The Original Cast of Characters

Our understanding of God's story—*our story*—and the cast of characters in this story can help us identify the characters in our individual stories, how they shape our perspective about us, about others, and about God.

After God's prelude to our story, when he designs the man and woman with an appetite for *More*—even in the middle of Paradise—and tells them they can enjoy everything except the fruit of the Tree-of-Knowledge-of-Good-and-Evil, a snake becomes a part of the cast. This wild and beautiful tempter tells Adam and Eve half of the truth about why God wants to deprive them of this one fruit. He slithers between all of the beauty in Paradise and tells them, "If you eat this fruit, you will be like God—you will be enough." That sounds good to Adam and Eve—if they just take an extra bite of Paradise, they can be in control of their own destinies! They forget God warned them that if they try to be their own gods, they will end up feeling empty and dead inside. So the snake betrays them and sets them up for shame, eventual homelessness, and empty wandering.

After trying to cover themselves with fig leaves, they finally stand face-to-face with God. My pastor says when we come face-to-face with God and think we can hide, it is like we're trying to cover ourselves with a fig-leaf bikini in the middle of a hurricane! Adam blames God and the woman God gave him for the mess. Eve blames the snake, and the snake slithers into the shadows. All this blame plants a crop of entitlement that includes the characters of relief, revenge, and evil. These characters make for a plot more outrageous than any found on reality TV. But God. God already cast himself into the story too. What a cast of characters!

- A passive man determined to relieve the tension.
- A controlling woman desperate for a scapegoat for the shame invading her own heart.
- An evil, conniving snake who seduces with half-truths and blinding beauty.
- A scary God who just might swallow them all up in the whirlwind of his anger—but who then covers them with the grace of a far less flimsy covering than fig leaves.

We're not much different in our own, modern-day stories. We are surrounded by characters who explain our choices to find comfort and control in an uncomfortable and out-of-control world, and we tend to blame everyone else in the story for our distress, for the creeping feeling of nakedness and shame. We console our longings with terrible stories filled with characters who abuse and abandon, or with glorious stories of characters who succeed and accomplish—all in the hope of making ourselves feel more palatable, either as sympathetic victims or triumphant overcomers. Eventually, this duality distorts our experience into proving or protecting, hiding or conquering, feeling pride or shame—making our stories so small because they become just about us. Entitlement makes relief and revenge our battle cries, while evil appears to win as isolation becomes our fortress. The result is we don't know what to do with the character of God. Is he silent? Careless? Watching? Our hearts hum along in desperation to the haunting words of Andrew Peterson's song "The Silence of God": "It's enough to drive a man crazy / It'll break a man's faith. . . . [There are times] when even followers get lost."[1]

Entitlement: *the sense that we deserve some relief from the tension of life or that we are justified in demanding revenge against someone for not giving us what we deserve. Entitlement leaves us bankrupt of all gratitude and authentic relationships.*

God's first story about us is a cautionary tale about the inevitable result of the merger of blame (I demand revenge) and entitlement (I deserve relief). It is emptiness, separation from God and each other, loss of identity and wholeness. Parker Palmer, in his book *A Hidden Wholeness*, explains further:

I have met too many people who suffer from an empty self. They have a bottomless pit where their identity should be—an inner void they try to fill with competitive success, consumerism, sexism, racism, or anything that might give them the illusion of being better than others. We embrace attitudes and practices such as these not because we regard ourselves as superior but because we have no sense of self at all. Putting others down becomes a path to identity, a path we would not need to walk if we knew who we were. . . .

. . . [W]hen community unravels and we lose touch with one another, the self atrophies and we lose touch with ourselves as well. Lacking opportunities to be ourselves in a web of relationships, our sense of self disappears, leading to behaviors that further fragment our relationships and spread the epidemic of inner emptiness.[2]

You only have to spend a few minutes on Facebook to know we are living in an epidemic of inner emptiness, complete with a cast of characters who escape in all kinds of "isms" or put others down as a path to their identity. But understanding the cast of characters in all of our stories—rather than blaming or dismissing them—can be a healing path *back to one another*.

The Character of Relief

The entitlement to relief shows up best in the genesis story of us in the character of Adam. Adam doesn't enter the potential tension of trying to dissuade Eve from taking the advice of the snake. He remains silent. When Adam comes face-to-face with God after eating the forbidden fruit, he suddenly has something to say: "I ate the fruit because of the woman you gave me" (Genesis 3:12, author's paraphrase). Adam wants relief from any consequences, and so he absolves himself of all responsibility. It's Eve's fault. It's God's fault. Before we get indignant about Adam, it's good to remember that whenever we seek relief from the pain and stress of life, we reveal this same deeper problem in ourselves. We don't want to get into the messiness of love.

The character who seeks relief may be an addict—addicted to drugs, working, sex, people-pleasing—desperate for relief from the reality of suffering. This character alternates between being oblivious and conscious of his or her pursuit of someone or something that will provide consolation from the longing for *More*. This is the character who looks for love in all the wrong places, the person who takes the easy way out (such as remaining silent or passive), the person who blames others or even themselves for their limitations to love or be loved and decides they are helpless to do anything about it.

This character is often tortured—like my client Tyler—by that inner voice whispering of *More*. This character may become numb, like Tyler's parents, through busyness, piety, or performance. This character may be like Tyler's peers, seeking the relief of being in a community of sameness that does not disrupt. This character can be active in all sorts of ways in an attempt to re-create a world that is better than the world that God put them in. Our longing for *More* gets distorted when we believe it's better to dissociate from reality, to let someone else take the blame, or to connect with a god (even if it's our own empty self) that might work better than a God to whom a day is like a thousand years (2 Peter 3:8, NIV). That God seems like a lunatic when we are frantic to find relief *now*.

Relief: *Radical pain is part of the human experience. The cry of pain is our deepest acknowledgment that we do not feel at home. Pain divides us from our true self, others, and God. We long for rest and do not trust it will ever come. The cry for relief is really asking God, "What are you doing?"*

We are all Adam. We all taste grief, fear, loneliness, and longing . . . and we all want relief. Whether we are passive, silent, avoidant, or addicted, the character who seeks relief discovers something that can dull the deepest passions of the heart to love and be loved. This character, although they may look passive, actually opposes love. The pursuit of relief nails the longings of our hearts to someone or something—a person, place, substance, behavior, or belief—that promises a little relief . . . and then we want more and more of it, until we are imprisoned in emptiness and self-hatred. Our attention is kidnapped by a desire to escape, and when our attention is held hostage, we cannot love.

No wonder Tyler was intrigued by a story about passion—as messy as the story of *The Passion of the Christ* is—filled with doubt, betrayal, loneliness, longing, grace, forgiveness, and love. Even as an eighteen-year-old, he knew that escaping his story did not soothe the longing that remained for *More*.

The Character of Revenge

Eve feels the longing for *More* even in Paradise, and the demand for revenge energizes her. She knows there is more than she can control, satisfy, and contain, and so when the serpent shows up and promises a remedy that is better than anything God offers, Eve is ready to bite. When God confronts her face-to-face, she knows already that something in her heart doesn't trust God. She knows that "something" is about more than wanting fruit. She knows that "something" promises god without God—and she knows the promise did not come from God. So Eve places the blame on the duplicitous serpent.

The character who wants revenge can look controlling, manipulative, driven, mean, and even murderous. This character often gets more press than the other characters because his or her actions are outrageous. As *The Big Book of Alcoholics Anonymous* says, these people live with "self-will run riot. . . . Driven by a hundred forms of fear, self-delusion, self-seeking, and self-pity . . . [they] step on the toes of [their] fellows."[3] This character wants revenge for the pain of life, for human limitations, or even for the limits set by God.

This character, like Tyler, may at one time or another renounce God or anything to do with God. This character, like Tyler's parents, may step over people on their way up the ladder to the good life. This character, like the peers in Tyler's story, may judge or reject anyone who is not like them. This character walks around with an internal clenched fist pointed to the heavens—furious, because if God were as he should be, he would not allow suffering, prejudice, heartbreak, dissension, or confusion.

> **Revenge:** *a hatred of our God-given desire for* More *in relationships, evidenced by distance, suspicion, or even an intent to do harm to anyone who might offer or ask for love.*

We are all Eve, energized by the force Parker Palmer suggests results in "unbridled competition, social irresponsibility, and the survival of the financially fittest . . . [and] community [being] torn apart . . . [and] depression—an extreme form of the empty self syndrome, an experience of self-annihilation just short of death." As a result of these grim symptoms, Parker explains, we commit selfish acts that "arise from an empty self, as we try to fill our emptiness in ways that harm others—or in ways that harm us and bring grief to those who care about us."[4] We are all bent in the direction of finding life on our own, despising any vulnerability or dependence. We don't want to have to deal with an economy of trust. We don't trust what God says about us. We don't trust each other. When we don't trust God, we must become god—even if it means we get stuck in the hard clay of the mire of ourselves. We end up with hearts of stone.

I'm not surprised Tyler's heart started to soften when he discovered he wasn't really alone. God had not abandoned him to himself.

The Character of Evil

Adam's desire for relief and Eve's demand for revenge put them just where the serpent wanted them. Evil wins when our hearts grow wary of one another and of God. The character of evil delights when our hearts become hard and love cannot break through. He slithers behind the scenes and suggests that we can be the most important character in our own stories, and he has a glint in his eye as he watches us decide we will make everything about us. The damage may look wild and beautiful (we are addicted to drama) and appeal to our longing for *More*, but in reality, our hearts are whispering or screaming, "No, God!" And evil is satisfied.

Some of us have stories with evil flesh-and-blood characters. A parent or someone in our lives who is committed to harm—maybe even enjoys the destruction. A person who is cold and has an inability to feel for other people. The flesh-and-blood evil character can be a full-blown narcissist—it is all about them: their ideas, definitions, popularity, problems, pain, needs. Or perhaps it's the person who is charming and gifted, who leads many, and who hurts just as many when they aren't so charming. In the past few years, we have felt defeated as one influential leader in the church after another have destroyed their lives through brutal, careless disregard for others. Many of us fear the church has become an "impostor factory," distorting the Good News of the gospel and consigning it to tell a very small story—a story committed to self-protection and self-preservation.

Evil people have more than just a hard heart—they have no capacity to feel shame over harming others. The greater the presence of evil in our stories, the greater the temptation to unconsciously mimic evil by hardening our own hearts to love. Trust and relationship seem crazy because evil has convinced us that neither is safe. We believe that allowing people in invites further harm. Evil twists our longing for *More* into wanting without engaging the tender, most alive parts of our hearts. Evil can overtake the characters seeking relief or revenge because it lies about all desire. Evil wants every character in the story to believe that if relationship is not escaped, then it must be destroyed.

Evil wants to slither between the cracks in all of our stories, but most of us are not evil. The character of evil still wins, though, when we believe our stories are only about us, when we can't see that our stories are actually stored in another story. When our stories are only about us, we can't see ourselves in others, and we don't let others see themselves in us. The result is that the image of God in us and in others is dimmed or distorted. As author and psychiatrist M. Scott Peck writes, "Evil . . . is characteristically inscrutable."[5] The character of evil wants to crush vulnerability, obscure transparency, and mock authenticity. Paradoxically, when I make it all about me, less and less of the real me is available.

Evil is revealed in Tyler's story in all the unspoken messages screaming in his head: *You are disgusting and unlovable. You can't trust anyone.* Evil is in the corners of Tyler's story when his parents' absence of real engagement makes room for the presence of the one who taunts him, mocks him, and cruelly sentences him to himself. Evil is slithering through the cracks in Tyler's story when he overhears his peers' gossip about someone else who doesn't "fit." Gossip delights in the murder of another's reputation, and that is evil.

Evil believes it's won—the story is over—when we are trapped in our own pain, fear, and confusion. We may have lied or cheated, driven under the influence, or had an affair, and evil wants us to think that's the real problem, so that we'll keep lying, denying there's a problem, or hiding our unfaithfulness. Adam and Eve's biggest problem was not that they ate the fruit. It was that they were ashamed and hid. They couldn't look at each other, and they couldn't meet God when he came to the Garden for communion with them.

My pastor says it this way:

When we betray, lust, lie, and retaliate . . . we
can't believe in God, for God is Love. . . . So I'm
convinced that your deepest problem is not the
sins you often commit, but what they lead you to
believe.

I'm convinced your deepest problem is not the
cigarettes you smoke, or the alcohol you drink in
secret; it's not the slander you speak or the gossip
you cherish; it's not the pornography you pleasure
yourself with; it's not the baby you aborted; it's not
that you betrayed your brother, cheated on your
bride, lied about the whole thing and retaliated with
murder. . . .

Your deepest problem is that somewhere deep
down inside of you, you believe that Jesus the
Messiah rose from the dead . . . just to kick your ass
[that's what a hard heart believes]. When, in fact,
He rose from the dead so you would believe that all
is forgiven, it is finished, righteousness and justice is
accomplished, and the Father is pleading with you,
"Come home. Come home!"[6]

As my wise client Kyle reminded me when I believed
that the character of evil was winning in my story, "Love
will have the final word." Evil does not have the final word.
DUIs do not have the final word. Sexual abuse does not have
the final word. Divorce does not have the final word. Our

self-destructive choices do not have the final word. We can choose to reject evil's power and lean into the most powerful character. As Andrew Peterson concludes in his provocative song, God has the final word: "The aching may remain / but the breaking does not."[7]

The Character of God

That brings us to the final character in our story. In the story of our genesis, Adam and Eve don't trust God with their hunger for *More*, and then they blame God for their choices. They try to write God out of the story, and I have sometimes wondered why God didn't just turn around and write them out of the story. Why didn't he just start a new story? Maybe the second time he could write a story where he creates a man and woman without choice—that way they wouldn't get into trouble. It astounds me that God lets us make choices, knowing that we might make bad ones. In fact, he gives us the right to choose because he wants us to choose. It's almost as if he already had something in mind to make those wrong choices right.

We get worried about the character of God because we don't understand how he can allow disaster—both natural disasters and relational disasters. What kind of character allows a child to be abused, a woman to be abandoned, or a man to utterly fail? What kind of a God deliberately designs a hungry man and woman, puts them in a garden with a fruitful tree right in front of them, and says, "You may be hungry, but don't eat from that tree"? That seems mean, even insulting, if not actually assaulting.

It reminds me of a story a friend shared with me. William started feeling terrible. His chest hurt, he felt sick to his stomach, and he was having trouble breathing. His wife, Dana, drove him to the hospital, and that's when his story starts to make no sense. Men and women in the hospital insulted him and told him that he was worse off than he thought he was. Then it felt to William like they assaulted him with probes and even knives. They knocked him unconscious, and they told his wife they didn't know if he was going to make it.

Tears come to my eyes as I think about my conversation with William. William did make it, and he called me from his home. I'm so grateful for those insulting and assaulting doctors, but probably not nearly as grateful as William is. They performed emergency surgery; drained fluid from his lungs and heart; opened up clogged vessels that were producing a hard, life-threatening heart of stone—and William left the hospital with a steadily beating, living heart of flesh.

When you feel insulted and even assaulted, it makes all the difference in the world who is thwarting your plans and who is cutting you and why they are cutting you. In our genesis story, Adam and Eve eat from the Tree-of-Knowledge-of-Good-and-Evil. Eve just takes a bite after the serpent lies to her and tells her she could be god if she knew enough to make her own judgments—that she could save herself *with* herself from the sometimes painful and confusing longing for *More*. She could be her own creator rather than God's creation. Adam is silent and passively agrees with Eve's decision while trying to remain unscathed by any scandal. They both eat the fruit and hide in shame, for they suddenly know good and evil, and they realize they've allowed the snake's lie to slither inside of them. Adam and Eve need something cut out of them. It's not their longing for *More*. It's their strategy to deal with their longing by being god without God. While looking for relief and revenge, Adam and Eve reached for a power that didn't belong to them. They tried to be god and ended up knowing more deeply than ever they were not God, so they hid from God.

As you think about the characters in your stories, who is most important? As a result of their presence in your story, is God more present or more absent? As a result of the characters in your story, what parts of yourself do you hide? Why? Do the characters in your story compel you to seek others or to stay stuck in yourself? Is the character of evil winning in your story? Scripture tells us the evil one comes *only* to steal, kill, and destroy (John 10:10). If the main themes of your story are you being "robbed," your hopes and dreams being killed, and any vision for the future being destroyed—evil has a leading role in your story.

When we review all of the characters in our stories, we come to a crossroads: What we believe about the character of God is the most important thing about us. Our view of his character shapes how we view our stories, how we interact with other characters, and how we give and receive belonging. How we view God determines whether evil takes a leading role—or God does.

What if, as Max Lucado writes, God is like a heart surgeon, and he needs to crack open your chest and remove your heart—poisoned as it is with pain (seeking relief) and pride (seeking revenge)? But God doesn't just remove your heart; he replaces it with his own.[8] That would mean God wasn't done making Adam and Eve in the prelude of the story when he designed them with hearts wanting *More*. He wasn't done making them when the cast of characters started acting out in the story he was writing. That would mean that he's not done writing your story, even if you've acted out of hurt or pride against God—even if you've decided he's not writing your story.

Whatever page you are on, God is still writing.

(into action)

1. Who is the most important character in your story?

- A parent or child?
- A spouse?
- Someone who betrayed you?
- Someone who loved you?
- You?
- The Enemy, who has stolen, lied, or destroyed?
- God?

2. Write a description of this character.

   - How does the character look?
   - What is their tone of voice?
   - How does the character enter a room?
   - What motivates this character?
   - What secrets does this character have?

3. Imagine inviting this character into the room with your jar of dust and broken pieces.

   - How would you tell this character about the painful places in your story?
   - Imagine this character holding one of your pieces of glass. What do you feel toward them? Toward yourself?
   - Is there a character in your story whom you can entrust your brokenness to completely?

   > Because our God is with us, we will be with each other. Because our God is on the throne, we will not spout off with each other but will be on our knees for each other. Because our compassionate God is all-powerful, we will be compassionate with each other, because this is the way of the most powerful. Because our God is close to the brokenhearted, we will be near to the hearts of all the broken of all of us.
   > ANN VOSKAMP[9]

CHAPTER 4

The Twist in the Plot

There is evil cast around us
But it's love that wrote the play
For in this darkness love can show the way.
DAVID WILCOX, "SHOW THE WAY"

FROM THE TIME MY SON WAS A TODDLER, he loved knives. He wanted to look at them, hold them, and talk about them all the time. He would have slept with a knife under his pillow if we let him. We had a really sharp knife, used to clean fish, that he especially loved. For his own protection, we hid that knife in a cupboard above the refrigerator. One afternoon, I walked into the kitchen and found that Graham had pushed a chair over to the counter, climbed on top of the counter, somehow climbed on top of the refrigerator, and retrieved the forbidden knife. When I walked into the kitchen, he was standing on the countertop, holding the knife.

I gasped. "Graham! You know you're not supposed to have that knife!"

Graham looked at the knife and then looked at me with mischief in his eyes. I couldn't resist. I uttered the words of mothers throughout the ages: "Graham, even if I had not caught you holding the knife, God would have known!"

The mischief quickly left his eyes as they filled with confusion. He cried out, "Mom, why is God always watching *me*?"

Why is God always watching us? We learn as children that God knows when we lie or pinch our siblings. God knows when we don't listen in church or when we laugh during Communion. When we reach adolescence, we learn that God is especially watching if we even think about sex, drinking, or drugs. Why is God always watching us? I'm afraid the impression we've been given is that we are the most important character in our story and God is watching so he can humiliate us, punish us, and whip us back into shape with his heavenly paddle.

What if that's not why he's watching?

In the genesis story of us, after Adam and Eve ate from the forbidden tree, God came to meet them in the evening. They were hiding—afraid of the plot of their stories. God looked at the Paradise he created, and on that morning, it was not good. Earlier in the story, God explained the one thing that is always "not good." In Genesis 2:18, God says, "It is not good that man should be alone" (NKJV). Whenever we are cut off from God and each other, we are at risk for misunderstanding our stories, making one chapter the whole story, and completely missing the plot twist—which means missing the plot entirely.

When God showed up in the Garden, Adam and Eve knew the truth. They couldn't be gods with dead hearts. They couldn't satisfy their appetites, and they couldn't get themselves out of the mess with the selves that got them into the mess. They needed God. It almost seems as if this was God's intention from the beginning: to create us with a hunger we cannot satisfy, even in Paradise.

Perhaps it's hard for you to entirely identify with Adam and Eve because you've never been in Paradise. Maybe, like me, the closest you've gotten is Disney World, and all we have to do to know we are a long way from Paradise is stand in line for three-and-a-half hours in ninety-five-degree Florida heat to ride Splash Mountain for less than ten minutes. Disney World is usually not the biggest disappointment in our stories. Acknowledging our appetite for *More* and the cast of characters that have come in and out of our lives provides the real evidence we are not in Paradise. Many of us stay stuck in not-Paradise, believing that's the end of the story.

But there's a twist in the plot. And in order to come to it, we need to examine our stories more carefully. Who is writing them? What do those less-than-satisfying chapters say about us, about others, about God?

> **Plot:** *"A tale with rich metaphor, mounting tension, character growth, plot momentum, and slowing, sweet resolve."*[1]

Examining Our Stories Is Essential

Examining our stories is essential to knowing ourselves because we *are* a story. Our lives are formed, twisted, and broken by a million little stories. Our stories reveal success and struggle, injustice and reward, despair and hope, failure and rescue. Most of us tell a story about ourselves inside our own heads, and seldom do we see ourselves clearly. Novelist and folklorist Zora Neale Hurston wisely warns, "There is no agony like bearing an untold story inside you."[2]

When our stories are buried inside of us, they can fester with shame, pride, anger, or despair. A man who hides his story of being sexually abused may come across as aloof or intimidating because we cannot see redemption of horror in our lives without the mirror of the redemptive stories of others and of God. A woman who lives in the shame of overeating may be telling her story of abandonment in life-swallowing ways, because we were not meant to bear grief alone. An adolescent who gulps down a bottle of pills to end her story may be filled with hopelessness because no one knows she needs to be rescued, and we were never intended to save ourselves. An unexamined life shackles us with a burden of pain, and carrying that burden day after day after day shapes us into men and women smaller, angrier, and more false than we were meant to be.

But there's more to examining our stories than our own personal growth and fulfillment. Our suffering and experience of betrayal and injustice help us understand God's story: writing his Son, Jesus, into the world to experience betrayal and injustice, becoming our rescue story. God knew we would experience stories filled with heart-scorching pain. He knew evil men and women would abuse innocent children. He knew husbands would say the life-altering words "I want a divorce." He knew women would drink, drive, and end up in handcuffs. He knew we would suffer in ways that would drain us, dismantle us, drive us or those who love us to our knees. God knew our million little stories and wrote the deepest story so our stories could be absorbed into his. Examining our stories of radical pain gives us a glimpse of what Jesus endured when he was crucified for the love of us. Our stories of recovery from addiction or restoration of a marriage from an affair reveal the glorious surprise of Jesus' resurrection. Our stories of transcendence over a crippling illness or the unspeakable loss of a child reveal Jesus' ascension, shouting his homecoming after all he suffered.

Without examining our stories honestly—laying them bare before trustworthy companions and God himself—we remain stuck in the unthinkable, inexplicable, and unredeemable. We will not grow into our true selves—men and women of clarity, compassion, courage, curiosity, and connectedness—if we don't tell the truths of our lives. We tell the stark raving truth, risk the eyes and ears of others on our stories, name the themes written into them, and do the hard work to allow our stories to form us into our true selves, because our stories reveal *God's* story.

When we start to tell our true stories, we sense that

everything in the story has meaning. What gives a story its meaning? Not the characters. Not even the plot. The author gives the story meaning. Once you get a hint of what the author is up to, there is meaning in every event in the story. The process of finding the meaning and trusting the author takes time, care, and courage.

Adam and Eve spent some time complaining about the Author of their story. He wasn't clear enough in his instructions. He left them alone. He was silent. He wasn't fair. Remember, this is *our* story. We are a paradox. We want God and we want to be god. We are proud and we are ashamed. We act and we throw others under the bus in blame for our actions. We fall down, we rise, and we hide. The result is the dismantling of belonging. Allowing our stories to lie dormant in us because we're afraid of what they might reveal makes us vulnerable to all kinds of traps that keep us away from our true selves, others, and God. We get caught in our capacity to deceive and our willingness to be deceived; in our love of power and using of people; in our striving for position and the shrinking of our souls; and in our clamor for privilege and silence at wrongdoing.

This is why God is always watching us: to catch us and show us we are not God, to rescue us from those traps, and to reveal *his* story in our stories. He gracefully uncovers the truth that our choices don't save us from the judgment of God; rather, the judgment of God saves us from our choices.

God called out to his creation, "Where are you?" God knew where they were, but his question is an expression of *his* appetite. The twist in the plot we often overlook is that God's hunger is greater than our own. He intends to be investigated for eternity, so he wove into the fabric of our souls a longing for *More*. He lets us try to satisfy that longing, and we inevitably end up in a swamp of emotions—arrogance, pride, manipulation, grandiosity, disappointment, betrayal, resentment, hurt, shame, and loneliness. He allows us to set out on our own to find answers to our deepest questions but remains committed to relentlessly reminding us, "It's not about you. It's about me."

> **Twist in the plot:** *For the better part of the story, we pick up clues and get to know characters, so we have a sense of how things are going to end. Then we discover our clues are false or our villain is in fact the true hero of the story. The entire direction of the narrative changes.*

The twist in the plot we often miss is that God doesn't want something from us. He wants us. *He* wants to be the Way back to belonging.

But to find the Way back, we must risk taking a closer look at our stories—especially at the chapters we've tried to forget, hide, or rewrite into more palatable content.

Examining Our Stories Is Painful

We miss the twist of God's longing for us because we don't take the time to really examine our stories. Make no mistake: Choosing to look honestly at our stories is painful. You may be feeling it right now because some chapter in your story is threatening to tip you over, and you're not sure you'll be able to get back up again. When I was in the depths of my alcoholism, every time I'd see a story in a magazine or memoir about a woman struggling with drinking, I'd turn the page or ignore the book. When a made-for-TV movie about alcoholism came on the screen, I'd change the channel. I was terrified that at best I'd be confronted with my own story and at worst I'd be exposed as the monstrous creature I thought I kept hidden from everyone else. The moment we consider honestly telling our own story is where evil is most effective in scaring us away from God, others, and even ourselves.

The pain of self-examination often compels us to manipulate the character in our story as either having too much power or too little power. There are many things in life—inside and outside of us—that we do not choose or control, that fall short of our ideals of perfection, and that we have a great deal of trouble accepting. As we work to accept rather than reject the realities beyond our control or outside our definition of perfection, our faith in the Storyteller can grow—but this pursuit can also initially lead to emotional suffering.

For example, we do not choose to be born; we do not choose the parents we are born to; and we do not choose the point in their lives we are born to them. We do not choose the parenting style of our parents (or that of their parents); we do not choose the trauma they endured before and after our birth; and we do not choose how their trauma history affects their parenting. We do not choose our parents' strengths; we do not choose their weaknesses; and we do not choose the parenting style we learn from them. In that sense, we do not choose how our parents teach us to parent ourselves, how they teach us to relate to our needs, thoughts, and feelings.

Much of how we think and feel is a result of who we are born to and when. We do not choose our ensuing psychological strengths, and, perhaps more regrettably, we do not choose our neuroses. This is an uncomfortable reality to face, especially in this age in which we strive toward images of perfection and we pride ourselves on feeling in control.

The chasm between our real-life stories and the stories we wish we were living can become the cliff we jump over with self-promoting or self-destructive choices, or it can be the place where we let go and fall into Love. When we see our stories as love stories, we experience "not good," so we want to choose the good of companionship. We come face-to-face with who we are not in order to long for the One who is called "I Am." We know the heartache of "not love" in order to want Love.

For a time, our stories may look like tragedies, filled with chapters we need to hide. But we will not be able to close the gap between the hidden self and our public self—we will not be able to experience wholeness—without examining our stories more fully. As author and psychologist Dan Allender explains, "Healing comes when I am willing to face the truth—deep and specific truth about myself. It is when my deepest desires are seen in light of what I can't do for myself. . . . Healing comes when our story is raw, bone-deep, and full of hunger."[3]

Examining Our Stories Takes Courage

I am sixty years old, and there are mornings when I look in the mirror and know that the best choice I can make is to turn off the light! I am shocked by the lines around my eyes. I try to hold up my chin so I don't see double. It is almost impossible for me to believe that my face reflects more of the God of the Universe than all the stars of creation. In fact, nothing else on earth is said to be made in the image of God—just you and me. That's why all our stories are creation stories. The Author creates us in his image and declares "everything is good." That's the plot.

We don't believe the plot is good when our stories are only about us. We can't see his image in us when our stories are only about us. Examining our stories with the belief they are all about us can be a bit like looking into one of those hotel mirrors that painfully reveals every crevice and blemish. We see in excruciating detail just how "not good" we are; how petty we can become when we don't get what we want; how mean we can be when others misjudge or hurt us; how capable we are of doing harm. We also see we were created with an appetite for *More* far deeper than we have imagined—and that can open the door to more pain, leading to self-contempt and self-rejection. It makes sense to us that the disappointment and heartache in our stories is the twist in the plot, and so we start to hate our stories—which means we miss our true selves.

> **False self:** *The self we project out of all the forces that constitute our lives—our genetic makeup, the nature of the man and woman who gave us life, the culture in which we were raised, people who have sustained us and people who have done us harm, the good and ill we have done to others and to ourselves, the experience of love and suffering—apart from God and his truth of who we are.*

Henri Nouwen wrote, "Self-rejection is the greatest enemy of the spiritual life because it contradicts the sacred voice that calls us the 'Beloved.'"[4] Do you reflect on your story and feel beloved? If your answer is no, perhaps it's because you've stopped before you came to the true twist in the plot. Maybe you don't know where to start, or shame seeps into the hem of you once you do start. Choose a story from a formative period of life to share with a trusted friend. Let your friend listen and feel your story with you, and then let them pursue understanding through conversation. Take it in. Maybe you can just tell one story. Start there.

Dan Allender encourages,

We were written not only to hear and tell stories, but we *are* a story. Our lives are composed of millions of stories, but most have been forgotten or simply don't register as important enough to remember. When I say that we are a story I'm saying that we're more than the sum of our stories. We are, in fact, a unique, once-on-the-earth life that reveals the story of Jesus in a fashion that no one else will ever do in the way we are written to reveal. If we fail to know the themes of our unique story, we are less likely to live that story well or play our role.[5]

After my DUI, I was compelled to reexamine my story. I wanted to know how I could be so selfish, if there were stories I'd forgotten holding clues to my struggle with addiction, and I started to wonder if my story was about more than me. I sure hoped it was.

What Sign Are You Wearing?

When I was a child, people would tell a story about me over and over again at family gatherings: "Sharon was so smart when she was just a little girl. She spent time with the neighbor who was from Italy, and by the time she was four years old, she could speak fluent Italian." I always wondered about that story. The story may have seemed charming to others, but something about it made me uncomfortable. I could no longer speak Italian, and I didn't feel exceptionally smart. In fact, I wanted to hide every time the story was retold.

When I was a toddler, we lived in a duplex apartment. We lived upstairs, and a single man who was from Italy lived in the basement. My mom was wrestling another toddler besides me. I know I escaped to the neighbor in the basement for attention and candy. When I was in his apartment, it was all about me, or so it seemed. I felt certain I orchestrated sitting on his lap to get the candy I wanted, and it only followed that I was responsible for the "icky" way he made me feel. The story of my Italian-language skills resurfaced shame I wore like a sign around my neck. Years later, a counselor remarked on how many hours I must have spent with this man to be able to speak fluent Italian. It was only in telling him this story that I realized the truth behind those uncomfortable, icky feelings. I was barely able to whisper the story lines from this chapter to my counselor: "He fondled me when I sat on his lap." I tugged at that *Shame* sign even harder. Why was I so stupid to go back to a predator time after time?

I didn't know then that the Author of my story allowed me to encounter "not good" so that I would hunger for something sweeter than any man on earth could give. God does not choose for people to inflict evil on us, but those horrors are not empty and void. God takes what is confusing and even perverse and plants a seed. A seed, even when planted in broken, dirty ground, carries the future in it.

When I was seven years old, we moved to Glenwood Springs, Colorado. I was the new girl in a new school, desperately longing to be a part of "the girls." I watched them every day at recess. They would link hands and chant, "Ticktock, the game is locked and nobody else can play but us, and if they do, we'll take their shoe and keep it for a week or two." It took me several days to work up the courage to offer my shoe to the ringleader of "the girls" and announce, "I want to play." The girls took my shoe and didn't let me play. I tugged at the *Shame* sign around my neck and went home that day afraid to tell my parents I was missing a shoe—and even more afraid to admit to myself I wasn't wanted. I started wearing another sign proclaiming, *I don't belong.*

The seed in my story grew roots and planted a hunger to be wanted deep in my soul. For a reason I can't explain (because I'm not the one writing my story), I started to lean into faith—believing there had to be more than just me to the story. As I recited Genesis 1:1 (NIV) in Sunday school—"In the beginning God created the heavens and the earth"—I wondered if my life was part of a bigger story being told. I didn't begin the story, and so maybe I wasn't the end of the story either.

When I was ten years old, I overheard my parents fighting for the first time. My mom was so angry and told my dad that as soon as the kids were grown, she was leaving. I was heartbroken and terrified. I snuck into my parents' bedroom while they were fighting, opened their closet, and for some reason, organized all of their shoes neatly on the floor. The next morning, my mom asked me if I'd organized the shoes. When I nodded, she smiled so big it soothed my shaky heart. "Oh, Sharon," she said, "you know how to make everything right." I started wearing another sign, one that was so heavy I could feel its weight rubbing against my neck. It said, *I am loved for what I do.*

I hoped that sign would guide me to a happy story, and so I excelled in all ways seen—straight As, president of the student body in college, married to a former president of the student body, mother to a beautiful girl and boy, owner of a well-decorated home in the suburbs. I added another sign just to remind me of my role in my story. This sign demanded, *Perform*.

I started writing books about relationships, and then my husband of twenty years told me he was lonely and had found a soul mate. My family broke into a million pieces all of the counseling and wisdom in the world could not put back together again. I added one more sign: *Rejected lover*.

I relapsed in my alcoholism (the *Alcoholic* sign seemed like it had never really been gone), and in the process, I hurt and scared a lot of people, including me. My son got depressed and tried marijuana. He told me it gave him a little peace. Who could blame him? My daughter became a cheerleader, got straight As, and was voted most likely to uphold the values of her Christian middle school. Eight years later, she told me she was an alcoholic. I didn't think twice about adding another sign: *Bad mother*.

My story seemed to announce other signs before I even put them on: *Vulnerable, Needy, Afraid, Pitiful*. After the DUI, I added a final sign: *I hate myself*.

I learned in Sunday school that "God is love," but my story didn't feel like a love story. The signs I wore chafed at my heart and put me in conflict with God and with the story he wanted to tell. I was experiencing the terrible reality of believing it was all up to me.

As I was piling on those signs, I didn't know yet that it was actually possible to be at peace with my stories—and as a result, at peace with the Storyteller. God does not leave us alone in our pain-filled chapters. In fact, the beginning of our story is sheer grace: He created us not because he needed us but because he wanted us. And he wants us still, and he will use every story to awaken our craving for him—if we find the courage to tell our stories. I often wondered how I would ever be brave enough to tell some of my stories, and then I read somewhere that the best way to become brave is to act like you're brave. I became willing to put on a brave face in desperation for a peace-filled heart.

When we are not at peace with our stories, we can't be at peace with the Storyteller. Unless we risk trusting that Grace is waiting in the ruins of our lives, we will hate those ruins and especially hate ourselves—our true selves, created by Grace. Bob Goff says, "Grace would climb stairs three at a time to get to us,"[6] but we need to show up at the top of the staircase, with our hands full of the dust and broken pieces of our stories, trusting God creates "very good" from dust and brokenness.

> **True self:** *the persistent yearning to be connected with some-thing—or someone—greater than our own ego, dust, and broken pieces.*

Maybe you're reading this and wondering why anyone would want to really examine their story. It *is* like looking into one of those unforgiving mirrors. Frankly, there are moments when I wish I didn't have to admit all I just wrote.

Yet, deep down beneath the signs I've worn, I know the stories they represent are significant. The evil one knows they are significant. The enemy of my soul has no desire for you and me to address the stories that have defined us—because in addressing them we get closer and closer to the character of God in our story.

Examining Our Stories Requires a Heart Broken Open to Worship

The core issue as we grapple with our stories is that ultimate question everyone who examines their lives asks at some point: "Where was God?" How can God let a four-year-old be sexually abused? Where is the God of the Universe while a family is falling apart? Why does God create us with an appetite for *More* and leave us feeling so lonely? Who is God? What is he about? What does it mean to trust him?

If we courageously examine our stories—especially our pain-filled stories—we have a few choices of how to respond: We can be ruled by relief and have a numb heart, dulled to the purposes of God in our stories; we can be ruled by revenge and have a hard heart, raising our fists against the purposes of God; or we will start to sense that there is a twist in the plot—and our hearts will be broken open to worship.

This is the paradox that occurs when we examine our stories in light of God's longing to love us: As we allow him to get closer and closer to the truths in our stories, we really don't see more and more of our flaws. Our failures are not the issue. What defines us is the Good News of God's unrelenting, adamant love for us. The closer we get to him as we tell the truth about our stories, the more he sees of what cannot be covered—and the more he sees, the more he loves us.

Our hearts can be broken open to God's love—even if our questions seem to have no good answers—because God doesn't ask us to cut up, smash, beautify, hide, or get rid of our signs. He is, however, intently interested in those signs.

A few years ago, as I was reflecting on my stories and asking some hard questions, I had a dream. Jesus was standing at the door of my apartment and knocking (that sounds kind of biblical).[7] In my dream, I peeked out the door, saw him, and slammed the door shut. I busily started to tidy up my apartment, just in case I changed my mind. He knocked again. I peeked out, and Jesus asked, "What are you wearing?" In one of those dream-mimics-life experiences, I looked down at my clothes to see if I was wearing mismatched shoes or an outfit from the '80s I kept in my closet for "special" occasions. And then I saw my signs, linked around my neck with worn, thick ropes. I was embarrassed and afraid, and I slammed the door again.

He didn't go away. A lifetime of wearing those signs made me want him to either invade my space or leave me because of the condemnation I felt. But he wouldn't leave. He simply waited. He waited, knocked again, and kindly said, "Sharon, here I am, knocking. If you invite me in, I will come in and be with you." *With* me? And my signs?

My lonely heart, filled with longing for intimacy, could not resist his kindness.

So, in the dream, I showed him my signs. He looked carefully at each sign, asked about the stories they represented, and with eyes full of tears, he asked to hold my signs. Still stuck in believing my story was all about me, I was afraid he'd use them as evidence against me. He then said the most unbelievable thing: "I'd like to take your signs. I've been waiting for this day since before the world began." *Take them where?* I wondered. *Waiting for what?* I imagined him taking them straight to my church to be displayed on the overhead screen in the sanctuary. What did he want with *my* signs?

"Sharon." He looked right into my eyes, and I knew he wasn't looking at me like the shame-filled, divorced, needy, alcoholic, pitiful woman I thought I was. He was looking at me with so much longing it took my breath away. "Sharon, I've been waiting to make your story mine."

This is the twist in the plot. The New Testament says that at the cross, Jesus wore a sign above his head announcing, *Jesus of Nazareth, King of the Jews.* It was written in several languages so everyone could read it. The sign was one of mockery—of disbelief. The oh-too-good-to-be-true news is that Jesus doesn't display our signs to condemn us, but he wears them to his death to make an intimate relationship with us possible. God's longing for us takes its ultimate form in Jesus' willingness to hang on a tree, stripped, naked, and bleeding for the love of us. He promises he will never leave us. He will descend into the hell of our stories to bring us Home to him, where we belong.

The Author of my story, the one who loved me first (1 John 4:19), created a choice in me before any other chapters were written. I didn't create the choice. But in gratitude, I chose to love him. And the seed planted in the dirty, broken ground of shame and self-hatred blossomed into a love story of being known and still wanted.

As you contemplate all that is true about your story, perhaps, just perhaps, this is the day you've prayed for: the day you stop trying to write yourself out of God's story and instead trust the Grand Storyteller of your life. God created this world, and he uses this world to create something in us. God knew that humans would choose to stay in shame and brokenness rather than risk coming out of hiding. The poet W. H. Auden says it this way: "We would rather be ruined than changed."[8] Although God doesn't choose our brokenness for us, he uses it to create desperation for him, for his meaning, his longing, his love. As Richard Foster wrote, "Today the heart of God is an open wound of love. He aches over our distance and preoccupation. He mourns that we do not draw near to him. He grieves that we have forgotten him. He weeps over our obsessions with muchness and manyness. He longs for our presence."[9] The twist in the plot has everything to do with God's longing to find us and become the Way back to our finding one another. As Richard Rohr wrote,

To put it another way, what I let God see and accept in me also becomes what I can see and accept in myself. And even more, it becomes that whereby I see everything else. This is why it is crucial to allow God and at least one other person to see us in our imperfection and even in our nakedness, as we are—rather than as we ideally wish to be. It is also why we must give others this same experience of being looked upon tenderly in *their* imperfection; otherwise, they will never know the essential and utterly transformative mystery of grace.[10]

Are you ready for a twist in the plot of your story? Can you believe God wants you even when you are good for nothing (Romans 5:6)? Do you want him when he seems like he is good for nothing—when he's not a vending machine, dispensing rewards based on your efforts (Job 13:15)? You are on the edge of a shift from "This is all about me" to "This is about us." And that will change everything.

(into action)

1. What signs do you wear as a result of your story?

2. Can you accept you are an unfinished story? God is still writing you. Does that make you feel hope or

despair? Why? What is your hope or fear in being "unfinished"?

3. Keep your eyes open for a "twist in the plot." Invite Jesus into the story with you. Consider these words from Dan Allender:

> Linger longer than you'd prefer in those moments where you felt shame. Shame is one of evil's most effective weapons to silence us and shut us down. It is where Satan divides our heart most effectively from God, others, and even from our self. Especially look at your sexual history even as a younger child and how the dark prince was thieving, killing, and destroying your integrity and joy as a man or woman. Look as well at what you know in your heart you don't really want to remember.[11]

4. What is the unique, once-on-the-earth life message that reveals the story of Jesus in your story? Dan Allender explains further: "The Good Story requires us to walk faithfully through each scene. It requires us to witness the violence of Good Friday, the disturbing details of which the gospels do not censor. It requires us to wade through the shadowlands of Holy Saturday, unsure and in between. And then it invites us to experience resurrection."[12]

5. Can you look at your jar of dust and broken pieces
   and believe it doesn't just represent the brokenness
   of your life, but the life of the One who was broken
   for you?

   > Grief is just so scary. Our grief and rage just
   > terrify us. If we finally begin to cry all those
   > suppressed tears, they will surely wash us
   > away like the Mississippi River. That's what
   > our parents told us. We got sent to our rooms
   > for having huge feelings. In my family, if you
   > cried or got angry, you didn't get dinner.
   >
   > We stuffed scary feelings down, and they
   > made us insane. I think it is pretty universal,
   > all this repression leading to violence and
   > fundamentalism and self-loathing and
   > addiction. All I know is that after 10 years
   > of being sober, with huge support to express
   > my pain and anger and shadow, the grief and
   > tears didn't wash me away. They gave me my
   > life back! They cleansed me, baptized me,
   > hydrated the earth at my feet. They brought
   > me home, to me, to the truth of me.
   >
   > ANNE LAMOTT[13]

CHAPTER 5

The Postlude:
Little Earthquakes
Everywhere

It is estimated that there are 500,000 detectable earthquakes in the world each year.
UNITED STATES GEOLOGICAL SURVEY,
WWW.USGS.GOV

When we die to something, something comes alive within us. If we die to self, charity comes alive; if we die to pride, service comes alive; if we die to lust, reverence for personality comes alive; if we die to anger, love comes alive.
ARCHBISHOP FULTON SHEEN, *PEACE OF SOUL*

"TODAY IS GOING TO BE ANOTHER RECORD-BREAKER." The news jolted me awake as my old-school radio alarm clock announced the start to another day. "Today will be the twenty-third day in a row we are above ninety degrees! There's not a cloud in the sky or a breeze in the air. Be sure to put on your sunscreen."

I hugged myself against the too-cheery weather spokesperson and shivered as I sat up in my bed. I couldn't explain it, but I felt a tremor. It seemed to me as if there was more going on beneath the surface of this still, summer day. My mind started to run over the schedule for the necessary tasks in my day, and then I stopped. Although I anticipated the daily work of seeing clients, paying bills, and figuring out what to eat for dinner, my heart was trembling with a deeper knowing of the real story line in my life: my daughter.

My daughter is in her early thirties. We have shared a relationship filled with joy and discord; beautiful memories and heart-shattering brokenness; mutual support and inexplicable estrangement. On that hot August morning, questions about Kristin filled my heart and mind: *Is she depressed today? Will she go to work? Should I call her? Did she read my text last night? How can I help her?*

I tell this story about Kristin with her permission, but it would probably be fairer to let her tell you about this chapter in her story:

> It started in college, innocently enough, as a way to study for the overwhelming number of exams and projects. I also found it helped me lose weight and ultimately feel like Super Woman. I thought I'd quit using after college, but my mind had already been hijacked. I came to believe that I needed it to do anything . . . even things as simple as relaxing on a Sunday afternoon.
>
> It's been a year since I've used stimulants, like Adderall and Vyvanse, and it's been strange. People who have known me but didn't know my struggle often remark that I seem "calmer." People who did know what was going on straight up tell me I'm

not as [crazy] anymore. Despite what [the years of drug abuse told me], I have been able to work, learn another language, go out with friends, exercise, and do many other things I thought I needed a "boost" to accomplish. But it's exhausting.

Even though it's been over a year, I still feel the effects of using stimulants for so many years. My body is still recalibrating, and I have to be patient with myself.[1]

Addiction shatters families. No one needs to tell me that. I can quickly recall hundreds of my own stories of addiction and see the trail of carnage left behind in the story of our family. I just never anticipated that my daughter would struggle. I guess I thought she would learn from my mistakes. Her addiction brought the unwelcome characters of Fear, Shame, and Anger right into the living room of my story.

I checked Kristin's social media daily and tried to decipher from her posts how she was doing, because there were some days when we were not speaking to each other. I read her post: *I'm breathing. I have been waiting my whole life for this.* My heart soared with hope that she was going to be okay. A few days later I read, *It's going to be a glass-half-full kind of day,* and wondered why. The next week she wrote, *Cheers to new beginnings and the magic they bring,* and I sighed, thinking of all the similar posts she shared before crashing into anxiety and depression.

Outside of Eden

The postlude to our genesis story is also one filled with fear, shame, and anger. Adam and Eve were escorted out of Paradise to engage in a world of painful relationships and to feel the futility of trying to make life work (Genesis 3:16-18). Pretty quickly, their world was shattered by one son murdering his brother. What a terrible time this must have been for Adam and Eve. Abel, their righteous son, was dead. Their firstborn son was a murderer. Their misplaced appetites for *More* first brought a separation between them and God, and then brought one between humans. The genesis story was widening and seemed to be plunging humanity into deeper and darker ways.

> **Futility:** *complete ineffectiveness.*

Outside of Eden, at every turn, we feel the loss in our relationships and efforts to make things work. Our hearts know, *This isn't right! This is not how it was supposed to be!*

Do you ever wonder what it would have been like if God just allowed Adam and Eve to stay in the Garden? They would still have lost the belonging they'd once known with each other and with God, but they'd be in Paradise. Wouldn't that be a better postlude?

Actually, that would have been the real tragedy in the story. That would be more like the captain on a sinking cruise ship deciding to make the passengers as comfortable as possible while the ship goes down, rather than disturbing their peaceful existence with blaring alarms. I don't know about you, but if the ship is going down—even if it's one of those fancy cruise ships—I want someone to unsettle and upset me.

The pain of relationships and the futility of trying to make life work is God's grace of letting us know that things are not how they're supposed to be. There's a deeper problem in need of a deeper story. God does not allow us to be comfortable in our alienation from him and one another. He doesn't want us to throw a party as the ship sinks. He allows desperation in the hope that we will find our way back to him and to one another.

My relationship with my daughter was a roller-coaster ride, and it shook the ground of my being, leaving cracks everywhere—cracks all too easily filled with dread, embarrassment, and fury. This was not the story I wanted. I pulled myself out of bed that August morning and started whispering lyrics from Tori Amos: "Oh, these little earthquakes / Here we go again . . . / Doesn't take much to rip us into pieces."[2]

On that hot summer morning, I did not know that the tremors of pain and futility I felt were cues of Grace that God uses to point us to the way back to each other.

The Epicenter and the Hypocenter

If you would have asked me, on that August morning, who was central in my life, I would have told you it was my daughter, Kristin. I would have been wrong. I needed some soul-shaking to name the truth.

The epicenter of an earthquake is the location of the quake on the surface of the earth. The truth about the epicenter of all that felt shaky in my life on that morning was *me*—my fear, my shame, my confusion, my wounds, and my anger. When we are central in our stories, we cannot love. We are largely mistaken about what true love really is. We think it's a feeling. It's not. As the poet Rilke wrote, "To love is good, too: love being difficult. For one human being to love another: that is perhaps the most difficult of all our tasks."[3] Love requires sacrifice, and that can be painful. When big feelings like fear, shame, and anger are central, sacrifice is the last thing the story is about. But earthquakes in our lives can shake our emotions into their proper place and prepare us to love.

Consider for a moment what love really looks like. Imagine someone knowing all about you. Everything. The things you are embarrassed about and don't want anyone to know. They notice everything about you, like that scar on your forehead. You hate it, but they love it because it's part of you. Imagine messing up, and even letting that person down. They forgive you. That's love. It's being fully known and accepted—not to just leave you as you are, but to connect you with someone greater than this world and to fill you with something (or someone) to offer to the world.

Rilke continued, "To love another . . . [is] the ultimate, the last test and proof, the work for which all other work is but preparation."[4] The difficulties in relationship with Kristin on the surface of my life were merely preparing me to love—real love that's embarrassing, messy, and almost always leaves scars.

The hypocenter of an earthquake is the location beneath the earth's surface where the rupture of the fault begins. The hypocenter in my life, again and again, has been God, disrupting me, shaking me, and breaking me to prepare me for a far deeper story. I started to sense the rumbling of God's preparation about two hours after the alarm clock jarred me from sleep. I walked outside of my office to bask in that August heat and take a quick break from clients and the chilling air-conditioning in my office. A Voice in the stirrings beneath the surface prompted me to call Kristin, though I wasn't expecting her to answer. She answered, and immediately her jumble of words started to splinter cracks throughout my epicenter.

"Mom, please don't be mad, but I took too much medication. I had all these bottles of blood-pressure meds that aren't working anyway and so . . . so . . . I just took them all."

My mind could not calm my shaking heart. I tried to understand, but she kept talking. "The paramedics are here. I think I'm fine, but . . ." Then there was silence. Maddening, deafening silence. I called her back, and there was no answer. I called again, and this time I could barely understand her. "Please don't be mad. They taking me to Presbyterian . . ." Her words were starting to slur and blur together. And then silence again.

I didn't know what to do. My car was at the repair shop. I had an appointment to get my hair cut in two hours. A client was probably waiting in the lobby. I could not stop shaking. I requested an Uber on my cell phone and fought back waves of fear and anger. *Did my daughter just try to kill herself? Was this for attention? What was she thinking?* I glanced at my phone and saw that the Uber driver would be arriving in two minutes in a Ford F-150 pickup. *Great,* I thought. I hate those trucks. They are hard for me to climb into, and then I knew I would have to sit right next to the driver, who would probably want to talk, and I was not in the mood for superficial conversation.

I was surprised when I saw the driver pull up in his bright-blue Ford F-150 pickup. He was an older gentleman dressed in a three-piece suit, sporting a chauffeur's cap. I climbed up in the truck and buckled my seat belt. I tried to calm my racing heart. The driver interrupted my thoughts and asked, "Is everything okay?"

"I think my daughter just tried to kill herself," I blurted out. It was the answer I didn't want to say or hear.

For the rest of the ride to Presbyterian St. Luke's hospital, my Uber driver sang. He drove carefully, kept his eyes on the road, and sang verses I didn't even know to accompany the familiar chorus: "Jesus, Jesus, how I trust him! / How I've proved him o'er and o'er! / Jesus, Jesus, precious Jesus! / O for grace to trust him more!"[5]

I don't remember the driver dropping me at the hospital. I don't remember climbing out of his truck. I'm not even sure he was human. As I look back now, I know God was beginning to graciously remind me I wasn't writing the story.

The Earthquake

As I walked into the hospital, it felt like a scene from the movies. Hospital personnel met me and rushed me into the emergency room. I strained to see Kristin through a sea of doctors and nurses. One doctor pulled me out into the hallway and said words I've heard on *Grey's Anatomy*, but never thought would be lines in my story: "Is there anyone you can call? Your daughter is very sick. We don't think she'll be able to survive this."

It is impossible to describe the next hours. I don't remember calling anyone, but people started showing up. The medical team moved Kristin to the ICU. I sat by her bed, held her hand, and sang the only words I could think of: "Jesus, Jesus . . . / O for grace to trust him more." I sat there for hours as family, friends, and strangers came in and out of the room. What I thought about most were the words I wished I'd said. My heart ached for a chance to be more intentional, to show and tell Kristin of my love for her. All the little earthquakes in our relationship separated us to the point where it seemed like we didn't even speak the same language anymore. I cried out to God, *I promise I'll learn her language. I'll become bilingual. Please don't let it be too late.*

The paradox of the earthquakes in our stories is they can compel us to let go of trying to be God, and in letting go, we find God himself. My story shifted dramatically from the 8:00 a.m. wake-up alarm to this midday chance to let go and let God be the Storyteller. Addiction, Shame, and Anger faded from the scene. Grace, Mercy, Trust, and Compassion became the most important characters in the story.

Two days later, Kristin woke up, and I was the one speaking a jumble of words. I told her I loved her. I asked her to forgive me for every grievance I could recall. I repented for allowing fear, shame, and fury to have prominent roles in our story. I knew all along I was in a stronger position to love well, but when I made the story all about me, I failed my daughter and failed to love.

In case you're wondering if I needed to wait for Kristin to acknowledge her mistakes and confess her vulnerabilities, you are missing the point of an earthquake. God allows cracks in our lives for us to let the Light in, not for us to push others into the crevices. An earthquake can be a disaster of darkness and doom or a movement toward Light and Love. After the devastating storm in Haiti, one survivor wrote:

> I know that many people will watch this devastation
> and register it in their "Why I know a good God
> does not exist" file. In my experience these moments
> of great thinning, traumatic cosmic brushes with
> mortality or instant poverty, are moments when the
> skin that separates heaven and earth is rent back to
> a translucent membrane. And it's easier to see God
> in those moments, not harder. He comes near to the
> scent of tears like a mother to her child's cries. The
> trees that still stand are getting barer by the moment,

but it feels like a party in my house. Meanwhile in America some people are so poor that all they have is money.[6]

The truly impoverished don't understand the grace outside of Paradise—the grace that makes us desperate for a redemptive Presence to move into the deep crevices of our regrets and failures. God writes earthquakes into stories to shake pinched, scared, paltry mothers like me into becoming extravagant lovers.

The Aftermath

I knew on that hot August day, in the aftermath of the worst earthquake I've experienced, that while I couldn't change the past, I was left with a clear choice going forward. That is the beauty of earthquakes. We can find clarity in the aftermath. First, I knew I had to own my mistakes. Honestly, I winced initially at this clarity. It seemed like a more painful option than Kristin owning her mistakes, but God's voice was clear after this storm: *Sharon, once you own your mistakes, they will no longer own you.*

It started to sink in. This catastrophe was not just a lesson in love; it *was* love. It was part of God's love story for Kristin and for me. These are some of the lessons God wrote into my story that day in ways I can never forget:

- **Be kind.** In the end, we won't care if we were right if we weren't kind, because "in kindness [God] takes us firmly by the hand and leads us into a radical life-change" (Romans 2:4).

- **Be generous in words and actions.** As I held my daughter's frail frame, tethered to the hospital bed by tubes and wires, God wrote lines into my story to lead to future chapters: *Never resist a generous impulse*, because we "are familiar with the generosity of our Master, Jesus Christ. Rich as he was, he gave it all away for us—in one stroke he became poor and we became rich" (2 Corinthians 8:9).

- **Create brave conversations—not to prove we're right but to extend olive branches, to offer reconciliation, to freely forgive, even if others refuse to own their part in the story.** Brave conversations are only possible to the degree God is the main character in our stories because "He didn't, and doesn't, wait for us to get ready. [Christ] presented himself for this sacrificial death when we were far too weak and rebellious to do anything to get ourselves ready. . . . God put his love on the line for us by offering his Son in sacrificial death while we were of no use whatever to him" (Romans 5:6-8).

- **Love is the character of transformation—not self-rightness, self-help, or self-sufficiency.** Our Storyteller is adamant in his love for us (1 John 3:1) and is adamant that we love one another (1 John 4:7). He promises, "You will be mine, and I will be yours. I will make an adamant promise, that I will not turn away from doing good for you. And I will put faith in me in your heart, so that you will not turn from me or others" (Jeremiah 32:38-40, author's paraphrase).

- **The characters in our stories we make our enemies are usually hurt people desperate to be loved.** Loving our enemies is not merely a biblical suggestion. Jesus tells us, "My command is this: Love each other *as I have loved you*" (John 15:12, NIV, emphasis added). This is a very good part of our stories. God is writing us to love as he loves us. We are not limited to how well the other characters in our story love us. At the end of the day, they are not our example for love. Jesus is.

God did not leave Adam and Eve or their descendants alone outside of the Garden. The postlude to the genesis story is this: *Outside of Paradise, the earth may shake; the ship may sink; families will be torn apart; countries will war against each other; there will be giants in the land; terrible people will be elected as rulers; floods will swallow the earth; famines will leave entire nations hungry; despite prophets, priests, and kings, the landmarks of faith, hope, and love will be covered up.*

You're going to need me, and we're going to need one another.

Loving one another is the postlude to our genesis story.

Before the summer earthquake in my story, I believed a relationship with my daughter was too painful and too hard. I didn't know that the heartache and the challenges were grace to show me the way back to the one who loved me, despite the pain and challenges of me, so that I could love others. The way back is filled with potholes and danger and inexplicable pain. It is populated with characters we'd just as soon write out of the story. The Way back is the one whose name is the Way (John 14:6, KJV)—the one who was alienated, misunderstood, judged, condemned, and crucified for us. His body was broken and blood shed to pay for the violation of his law in the Garden and to ratify his new and eternal covenant of grace. He chooses to be bound to us by his own eternal nature of adamant love. God's love also binds us all together in a covenant, and Jesus shows us the soul-shaking way back to finding one another.

The way back reminds me of a familiar childhood story. Let's read it again, thinking about our way back to becoming real:

> "What is REAL?" asked the Rabbit one day, when they were lying side by side near the nursery fender, before Nana came to tidy the room. "Does it mean having things that buzz inside you and a stick-out handle?"
>
> "Real isn't how you are made," said the Skin Horse. "It's a thing that happens to you. When a child loves you for a long, long time, not just to play with, but REALLY loves you, then you become Real."
>
> "Does it hurt?" asked the Rabbit.

"Sometimes," said the Skin Horse, for he was always truthful. "When you are Real you don't mind being hurt."

"Does it happen all at once, like being wound up," he asked, "or bit by bit?"

"It doesn't happen all at once," said the Skin Horse. "You become. It takes a long time. That's why it doesn't happen often to people who break easily, or have sharp edges, or who have to be carefully kept. Generally, by the time you are Real, most of your hair has been loved off, and your eyes drop out and you get loose in the joints and very shabby. But these things don't matter at all, because once you are Real you can't be ugly, except to people who don't understand."[7]

The way back is the love of God, the heart of God, the Son of God—Jesus, loose in the joints and kind of shabby (check out Psalm 22:14!), crucified for the love of us. God uses painful, difficult relationships to make us real, in the image of Christ, to help us find the way back to one another.

But so often we try to find other ways back, don't we?

When I was a freshman in college, one of the big events of the school year was the Valentine's Banquet. I could not wait! I dreamed of a handsome date, a breathtaking dress, and a beautiful corsage, but as the date approached, I had not been asked.

At the college I attended (way back in the Dark Ages), we

were required to eat dinner in the dining hall, and we were assigned to tables—four men and four women at every table (to help the dating process along). One night after dinner, I sensed someone following me closely out of the dining hall. I stopped and came face-to-face with one of the men from my table. Jim was kind of a nerd and probably not the most sought-after man on campus (but apparently, I was not the most sought-after woman).

Jim stuttered, "Um, Sharon, um, I mean, Sharon, will you, will you . . . go to the Valentine's Banquet with me?" I wasn't sure whether to feel relieved or reluctant, but I answered, "Yes!" And Jim replied, "Whew! I've asked every other girl at the table."

Humiliation floods me as I recall that story, but I know now it was a little earthquake. It was not only a lesson about love; it *was* love. Every time I recall that chapter in my story, I think of all the times I've asked everyone else at the table to be my source of Light and Love. Every earthquake has taught me that God waits patiently for me, and what astounds me most is that he never gets tired of waiting—and he is never ashamed that he asked me first.

> **Humility:** *the opposite of making life all about me. In the words of the poet Rumi, "Discard yourself and thereby regain yourself. Spread the trap of humility and ensnare love."*[8]

The terrible, beautiful earthquake on that hot August day shook both Kristin and me to get busy living—in our individual stories, in our together story, and in the stories of others. We started to see that every earthquake is meant to shake us in our depths to know this truth: "This is the Story in which you have found yourself. Here is how it got started. Here is where it went wrong. Here is what will happen next. Now this—this is the role you've been given. If you want to fulfill your destiny, this is what you must do. These are your cues."[9]

Mother Teresa once said, "If we have no peace, it is because we have forgotten that we belong to each other."[10] What could change if we remembered?

The terrible, beautiful earthquake was a prophecy of more earthquakes to come. Earthquakes that would throw me into the wayback, unearth further changes in me—shaking me out of safety, freaking me out a little, and surprising me with not only the wild goodness of God but the wonder of companionship.

(into action)

1. Write out the story of a recent "earthquake" in your life. Who is at the epicenter? Why do you believe God allowed this earthquake? What lessons have you learned about love in its aftermath?

2. Look at your jar of dust and broken pieces. What earthquakes caused those ruins? Whom do the pieces belong to?

3. Maybe you're in the middle of an earthquake now. In her book *Little Earthquakes*, Jennifer Weiner describes the experience:

> I could feel my knees and neck wobbling, as if they'd been packed full of grease and ball bearings. I set one hand against the wall to steady myself so I wouldn't start to slide sideways. I remembered reading somewhere about how a news crew had interviewed someone caught in the '94 Northridge earthquake. *How long did it go on?* the bland, tan newsman asked. The woman who'd lost her home and her husband had looked at him with haunted eyes and said, *It's still happening.*[11]

If it's still happening in your story, you might have no idea why God allowed this chapter in your life or what the lessons are in the aftermath. Consider taking a few of the pieces from your jar and sharing some of the earthquakes you're experiencing with a trusted friend, trusting that God is, as author Bob Goff says, "more interested in making us grow than having us look finished."[12]

I had my own notion of grief.
I thought it was the sad time
That followed the death of someone you love.
And you had to push through it

To get to the other side.
But I'm learning there is no other side.
There is no pushing through.
But rather,
There is absorption.
Adjustment.
Acceptance.
And grief is not something you complete
But rather, you endure.
Grief is not a task to finish
And move on,
But an element of yourself—
An alteration of your being.
A new way of seeing.
A new dimension of self.

GWEN FLOWERS, "GRIEF"[13]

(common grace)

PART II

*Astonishing material and revelation
appear in our lives all the time. Let it be.
Unto us, so much is given. We just have to
be open for business.*
ANNE LAMOTT, *HELP, THANKS, WOW*

CHAPTER 6

Changing You in the Story

Yesterday I was clever, so I wanted to change the world. Today I am wise, so I am changing myself.
RUMI

IT WAS AN ORDINARY FRIDAY NIGHT after small group at church. Everyone sprawled around the tables at Starbucks with their Frappuccinos and cold-brew lattes. Then one of the men in our group, Jake, tripped a political land mine:

"I just don't understand how you can be a Christian and not support our president. I mean, this wall he wants to build is to protect us. How can anyone be against that? And the Democrats are idiots for delaying the process—causing a government shutdown."

Jake seemed to be looking for a debate. I wondered if maybe he was hoping for a real dialogue—wanting to be seen, to be heard, to feel a sense of belonging. I knew he'd never admit it.

"Well, the Bible doesn't share your perspective," Haley, another participant in our small group, quickly offered. "Jesus has always been welcoming to immigrants and outcasts. I don't see how you can be a Christian and be for a wall that keeps people out."

Jake met Haley's jab with one of his own: "That's incredibly naive, Haley. Do you know the statistics about the destructive behaviors coming through the border and how they affect us—our crime rates, taxes, and illegal-drug issues? This isn't even about being 'Christian.' Try thinking and being intelligent instead of just spouting the latest nonsense from NPR."

Haley was stunned a little by the personal attack, but she couldn't stop. She's like the rest of us. Over 75 percent[1] of social-media interaction is generated by well-meaning people who take their passionate opinions into relationally violent conversations.

Relational violence: *harm expressed through direct or nuanced beliefs; language and behavior including demeaning, dismissive, and demanding messages. Relational violence also includes complete withdrawal from relationship in the midst of dialogue.*

"Jake, I care that families are separated. I care that evangelical Christians are failing their call to love and to be healers and compassionate caregivers to the poor and invisible. It is too bad marginalized people don't benefit from your passion. That offends me!"

Some in our small group nodded. Others, like me, remained frozen, looking into their coffee cups. Most wandered into different conversations. Jake walked out.

When adamant and conditional ugly conversations become the postludes to our stories of being loved adamantly and unconditionally by God, we end up pulling and pushing, shaping and deforming what we believe about God, ourselves, and one another. Our culture has become fragmented and angry, and that means we face significant barriers to the way back:

- According to Barna Research, today there are more adults in the United States who don't attend church regularly than those who do.[2]

- One woman tells her real story, reflecting Barna's research: "I didn't become a Christian because of the man who carried the cross down the strip of Panama City Beach yelling. I didn't want Jesus because the girl all put together in high school told me I needed Him. And I SURE didn't give my life to Christ because of the girls at a church who laughed at me when I was sick in the bathroom with a hangover."[3]

- Relational violence starts early. Studies suggest that by the time a girl in the United States is a teenager, she will be called a variety of harmful and derogatory names— often on a daily basis.[4] The profane culture is not that different for boys.

- According to a worldwide Stage of Life survey of teens, "97% of students learn their manners from home," and "57% [of survey respondents] learn manners and civility from their place of worship."[5] Lessons in civility are failing as families reflect our fragmented culture and their individual members go to their own rooms to be on their individual devices with little accountability for their interactions with others.

- Engaging in websites that serve to replace normal social function is linked to psychological disorders like depression and Internet addiction.[6]

- Social anxiety "affects approximately 15 million American adults," depleting and diminishing human interaction.[7]

- The failure of our stories to cultivate Christlike love results in a lack of empathy and draws dividing lines between political parties,[8] skin pigmentation, and lifestyle choices.

- Evangelical Christians draw the most dividing lines, and as a result, according to one author, "fewer and fewer Americans identify with any particular denomination. About a third of millennials have no religious denomination, and some studies indicate that about half of Generation Z has no religious affiliation. 26% of people over 65 identify as white evangelical, but only 7% of people under 30 do."[9]

These statistics matter to me because they are about me and my children. *Do I live in a way that makes anyone, much less my children, curious about why I go to church? Is the way I'm living drawing people back toward wholeness—or pushing them (and me) further away?* One author summarizes the dismay many of us feel about the fallout from conversations like the one I described occurring after my small group met:

> Over the past two years, as our American political process unfolded, and as respected and high-profile evangelists and preachers and Christian speakers endorsed candidates and took to social media with ever more bigoted, hateful, alarmist claims—and as millions of pledged Jesus followers gleefully rushed to celebrate and defend and accompany them in their crusades, I've come to find myself estranged; pushed to the furthest periphery of "God's people."[10]

You may be able to debate every statistic and quotation I've listed, but how do you answer the sixteen-year-old boy who sat in my counseling office and asked, "Why would I have faith or trust love when I can't find any real evidence of it at home, school, or church?"

In our modern culture, many of us have been re-programmed. We don't know how to have real conversations representative of our beliefs while being kind and respectful of others. We have been programmed to talk (or post) about what grabs our attention for a few minutes and then move on—often leaving behind a trail of missed connections and hurting people. We don't know how to shape our interactions in ways that reflect our stories of being loved by God. We don't invite others to belonging, to finding grace in the postlude of our stories. Instead, we invite others to debate or be left behind.

Relational reprogramming: *"We have created tools that are ripping apart the social fabric of how society works."—former Facebook executive*[11]

"Our time has been called the 'age of loneliness.' It's estimated that one in five Americans suffers from persistent loneliness."[12] Our stories of being created by Love and for love are lost in translation in our unhealthy relational patterns with one another. As Diane Kalen-Sukra notes, "Incivility is the social equivalent of CO_2 and leads to a sort of cultural climate change that is very difficult to reverse. Anger, confusion, and a willingness to engage in bullying to get one's way; these are all results of the current hot house climate we find ourselves in."[13] How can we change the climate—or the story—so we are connected to the deeper story of love the Grand Storyteller of our lives wants us to tell?

I thought about the conversation I heard after small group in Starbucks and easily identified Jake as someone who needs to change. He needs to get in touch with why he tripped a land mine to begin with and why he couldn't hang in there to see a resolution in the conversation. I decided (without asking him) that he probably has unresolved trauma and needs to see a good therapist to learn about emotional intelligence.

I also thought it would be good for Haley to change. She talked about compassion and care but did not demonstrate it when she lashed out at Jake. I quickly decided (without talking to her) that Haley is probably part of the self-righteous in the church who offend so many and keep those millennials and members of Generation Z from identifying with a church. She needs to repent and spend some of her healing grace on Jake.

But during my reflections on the horrible conversation after small group, I started to feel the tremors of an earthquake. Why didn't I say something to turn the conversation? Why didn't I ask Jake why this topic was important to him? Where was my compassionate insight or empathetic gesture? Why didn't I ask Haley why she was personally offended?

I remembered (and was caught by) the challenging words of Donald Miller quoted by Dennis Okholm in *Monk Habits for Everyday People*:

> More than my questions about the efficacy of social action were my questions about my own motives. Do I want social justice for the oppressed, or do I just want to be known as a socially active person? I spend 95 percent of my time thinking about myself

anyway. I don't have to watch the evening news to see that the world is bad, I only have to look at myself. . . . I was the very problem I had been protesting. I wanted to make a sign that read, "I AM THE PROBLEM!"[14]

Dennis's reflections on this quote are startlingly honest:

Such Christian humility is not the same thing as low self-esteem or poor self-image. It is simply the refusal to be deluded by the lie that I am guiltless.[15]

Could I admit the truth? In allowing personal offense or fear to keep me out of the conversation, I had forgotten my own story, and I had lost the opportunity to connect our collective stories to God's story and facilitate an environment of grace.

The Gift of Common Grace

It is easy to point fingers at the loudest voices in the divisive conversations fragmenting our world. I can clearly see how *their* understanding of God's love story does not translate into their daily human stories, but that night at Starbucks, I was guilty of relational violence too. I was offended by the derogatory remarks and didn't agree with either opinion wholeheartedly. I was afraid of being splintered with shrapnel if I got involved.

Sociologists underscore that my response is not unusual.

Fear is so pervasive that experts have made the case that we live in a generalized "culture of fear": "This fear factor breeds more violence, mental illness and trauma, [and] social disintegration."[16]

When we forget our stories of rescue and love, we step into the aftermath of self-absorption, as author and philosopher Baltasar Gracián poignantly describes: "He that has satisfied his thirst turns his back on the well. . . . When dependence disappears, good behavior goes with it as well as respect. . . . Let not silence be carried to excess lest you go wrong, nor let another's failings grow incurable for the sake of your own advantage."[17] Being offended or afraid in the midst of tricky conversations denies common grace and turns our back on the well of Grace that has slaked our thirst for love and belonging.

But as we live within the story of God and alongside the stories of others, we will learn to see **common grace**—ribbons of God's good and perfect gifts in every interaction and every relationship. Common grace, according to author and theologian Tim Keller, is "a desire on God's part to bestow certain blessings on all human beings, believer and nonbeliever alike."[18] Without common grace, every conversation can become a curse that reveals badness, foolishness, injustice, and ugliness. But when we begin to understand our stories and listen to our lives, we start to recognize every conversation as a gift that can reveal goodness, wisdom, justice, and beauty.

Common grace requires humility. Humility is a way of

being in the world—knowing that an ability to write or bake or manage money is a gift; a sense of timing or intuition is a gift; the skill to paint, make music, or act is a gift. When our child makes the varsity baseball team, that is a gift. When we make a wise parenting decision, that is a gift. When we save an extra five thousand dollars, that is a gift. When we celebrate twenty-five years of marriage, that is a gift. When we are the beneficiary of someone's kindness, that is a gift. When we encourage someone, that is a gift. When someone challenges us, that is a gift. All is grace.

Perhaps this is the world the apostle Paul imagined when he wrote, "In Christ's family there can be no division into Jew and non-Jew, slave and free, male and female" (Galatians 3:28). Imagine a world where every human interaction is viewed as a gift—where there is no distinction based on ethnicity, philosophy, socioeconomic demographics, or gender because everything we have is a "gift . . . coming down from the Father of the heavenly lights" (James 1:17, NIV).

An environment of common grace creates a world where there is no room to be personally offended, no need to be afraid of engaging with others, and no value in hammering at different topics with dogmatism to prove we are right. Rather than turning anyone away in condemnation or uncomfortability, when we advocate for the dignity of common grace, we see every conversation as a gift, every perspective as a gift, and every person we encounter as a gift. We begin to *anticipate* conversations as ways to expose the brilliance of God's love instead of our own brilliance. We can have conversations on any topic and with any person, trusting God himself will use every interaction to deepen our collective hunger for love.

Do you believe God has granted you thousands of gifts—that *you* are a gift? We will not be able to change a relationally violent conversation into a graceful conversation unless we know—heart and soul—that all we are and have is a gift. We won't be able to seek out difficult people, arrogant people, narcissistic people, or hurting people unless we believe *they* are a gift and trust God's gifts to us to be our offering to others.

All too often when we participate in or observe difficult conversations, we forget that real people are involved. When the interaction becomes about our ego, our reputation, our fear, or our personal offense, it is hijacked by a distorted and damaging view of the *reason* we discourse with others in the first place—finding the Way back to belonging. Remember the time you proved your rightness and others asked you to tell them about Jesus? Me neither.

It's Only a Bagel

Earlier this week, I stood in line at Einstein Bros. Bagels for my morning treat of a perfectly toasted cinnamon raisin bagel slathered with peanut butter. The line was not moving. I looked at my watch and noted I had twenty minutes to get to work. I sighed loudly and looked at the man in line behind me for some commiseration. He was dressed in an expensive suit and polished wing-tip shoes. I thought he would get it.

He's busy, like I am. I mumbled under my breath, "You'd think they could have more than one person behind the counter." The line remained still. I started tapping my foot and making louder disgruntled noises. "I don't know how hard it is to get someone who can slice a bagel."

The important-looking man behind me spoke softly: "I think this may be her first day."

I did not take a cue from his kind tone. I continued, more loudly, "Well, you'd think they'd know not to train her during the busiest time of the day." By this time, I didn't care who heard me. I was certain everyone else was just as outraged as I was. But then the man behind me—suit, starched white shirt, polished shoes, and all—did the most surprising thing. He jumped over the counter and said to the bewildered new employee, "It looks like you can use some help. Just tell me what you want me to do."

The dialogue in the line to get bagels was certainly not as significant as the politically charged conversation after my small group. Or was it? If any of the other people in line or behind the counter were hungry for more than bagels— hungry for acceptance, mercy, connection, meaning, or grace—who do you think they'd want to talk to? Me, with my self-rightness plastered all over my face? Or the man from behind me in line, who now had cream cheese smeared on his fancy suit?

Common grace believes that every interaction with any-one could be the moment we get to turn the world upside down by making that moment about care, graciousness, peace, kindness, hope, a sense we don't have to take ourselves so seriously, and a conviction it is not all about us. Before we can change the conversation or invite others into the conversation, we need change in *us*—deep down where offenses are cultivated, fears grow, and what we really believe about God is revealed.

The High Cost of Being Personally Offended

Many of us are deeply offended by political and philosophical realities in our world. We are concerned about people's perceptions. We are deeply concerned about people's sinful choices. We are personally offended by people's words and actions. Relational violence grows out of personal offense and is a wound on society and individuals.

> **Personal offense:** *a rigid sense of who is "in" and who is "out."*

Being personally offended comes with a high cost. I have friends whose son died from AIDS, and they were left alone because their church community didn't know how to respond. I walked alongside a client whose husband walked into her hospital room shortly after the birth of their first child and announced he was leaving her for another woman because he was offended by his wife's beliefs. One woman in my recovery group sat in silence for weeks before she dared ask the question burned into her heart by careless comments from religious people: "Do you think I'm going to hell because I'm addicted to heroin?" A thirteen-year-old girl recently confessed to me she had no one to sit with at lunch because she supported our president and was on the unpopular side of the line drawn in her middle school.

What does it mean when we are personally offended? We believe someone else's beliefs, actions, or affiliations have violated our rightness. More than just saying someone is wrong, being personally offended reveals we believe someone has wronged *us* and needs to give an account to us because we are the judge.

I am convicted by the words of the Trinity in *The Shack* when they describe the process of letting go of personal offenses:

Life takes a bit of time and a lot of relationship.[19]
PAPA (GOD THE FATHER)

The truth shall set you free and the truth has a name. . . . Everything is about *him*. And freedom is a process that happens inside a relationship with him. Then all that stuff [personal offenses] . . . churnin' around *inside* will start to work its way out.[20]
PAPA (GOD THE FATHER)

When all you can see is your pain, perhaps then you lose sight of [Truth].[21]
PAPA (GOD THE FATHER)

You must give up your right to decide what is good and evil on your own terms. That is a hard pill to swallow—choosing to live only in me. To do that, you must know me enough to trust me and learn to rest in my inherent goodness.[22]

SARAYU (HOLY SPIRIT)

I don't want to be first among a list of values; I want to be at the *center* of everything. When I live in you, then together we can live through everything that happens to you. Rather than the top of a pyramid, I want to be the center of a mobile, where everything in your life—your friends, family, occupation, thoughts, activities[, conversations]—is connected to me but moves with the wind, in and out and back and forth, in an incredible dance of being.[23]

JESUS

Rather than being rooted in personal offenses, we're invited into a dance in celebration of common grace. The next time you are personally offended, read these words. They might reveal what being personally offended is covering up:

If you think that leaves you on the high ground where you can point your finger at others, think again. Every time you criticize someone, you

condemn yourself. It takes one to know one.
Judgmental criticism of others is a well-known
way of escaping detection in your own crimes and
misdemeanors. But God isn't so easily diverted.

ROMANS 2:1-2

Our sins nailed Jesus to the cross, where he bore hell for
us. All our offenses were laid on him (Isaiah 53:6)—our
DUIs, gossip, envy, little white lies, big gaping lies, fudged
income-tax returns, relational violence in the line at Einstein
Bros. Bagels. Once we've stood before the crucified Savior
and embraced his story, it's hard to be personally offended
by someone else.

The Kingdom of truth, beauty, and goodness does not
come by convincing people we are right at any cost or by
cramming our truth down someone's throat. The Kingdom
of truth, beauty, and goodness comes through something
much more powerful than our attempts to persuade. Jesus
set the Kingdom in motion when he was crucified, and he
invites us into the building of that Kingdom with these
words: "If any of you wants to be my follower, you must
give up your own way, take up your cross, and follow me"
(Matthew 16:24, NLT). The Kingdom is about letting go of
another person's throat.

What if we entered every conversation with a cross
on our backs? Before we file that away as a platitude, we
need to remember crosses are for getting crucified by those
who hate us because we love them. Crosses are for bearing

another person's hell. Crosses are for carrying another person's wounds—sometimes the wounds of those who have hurt us. *Love always leaves a mark.*

It's easier to be personally offended than it is to be crucified. It's easier to be personally offended than to invite someone you don't understand or approve of to lunch. It's easier to be personally offended than to ask questions. It's easier to be personally offended than to risk getting involved with people who might hurt you. But instead of cultivating offenses, do we have the courage to pick up a cross?

Pastor and author Phil Vaughn describes how "picking up a cross" and being willing to die to ourselves can resurrect something new and change who we are in interactions with others:

> What if the problem isn't really the issue? What if
> my perspective is the problem . . . the way I see it.
> In other words, what if what I think I know is in the
> way of what I need to learn?
>
> I've spent the last couple of weeks pondering the
> conversation between Jesus and Nicodemus in John 3.
>
> Jesus tells Nicodemus that if he wants to see the
> Kingdom of God he needs to be "born again."
>
> What an intriguing phrase.
>
> It seems as if Jesus is telling Nicodemus to:
>
> Start over. Begin again. Forget what you think
> you know, Nicodemus. It's in the way of what you
> need to learn. You can't see "new" because of the

"old." Listen with new ears. Challenge your currently held assumptions. The structure that got you this far is now in the way. . . . Dismantle it with gratitude and embrace the New Thing that God is doing.

Start over and approach this as a beginner . . . as helpless and innocent as a newborn infant—be born again. Only then can you see the unimaginable grace and mercy of an all-loving God who is leading you to new places.[24]

The Trap of Fear

The boundaries of personal offense may seem neat and tidy with clear lines of who is right and wrong, in and out, acceptable and suspect—but being personally offended will always paralyze us between those lines in the trap of fear. It's a trap because dividing lines never give us answers to the deep questions of the heart. Dividing lines will never love us. Dividing lines are the way out of belonging.

When I found myself frozen in fear during our small-group conversation, I was afraid of the loud personalities or that I'd say the wrong thing—either falling flat on my face in foolishness or further fanning the fire with my comments. When we are in the trap of fear, we will never feel the freedom of love. We step out of the trap as we acknowledge the difficult characters in the conversation and remember the reason for the conversation: to create belonging connected to something more than us, not a following that's about us.

We all have to deal with difficult people. Recently, I was discussing my fear of posting on social media with a friend. I told him, "I'm just afraid of the trolls—the people who condemn, criticize, and put me in a box of their judgment." My friend admitted to me he, too, was afraid of trolls until he realized he was the troll. Sometimes the difficult people are us. As we deal with difficult interactions, our own frustrations and flaws are exposed.

Troll: *when we post a deliberately provocative message or intend to cause an argument.*

In *The Shack*, the protagonist expresses his frustration with difficult people and the ensuing fear that captures him. Jesus answers, "All I want from you is to trust me with what little you can, and grow in loving people around you with the same love I share with you. It's not your job to change them, or to convince them. You are free to love without an agenda."[25]

It's not our job to change people.

It's not our job to change people.

It's not our job to change people.

The goal is not to get someone to be less difficult. The impossibility of that task lights a match to our personal offenses or sends us away, scurrying into the trap of fear. Freedom from frustration and fear includes flexibility, tender strength, and endurance fueled by forgiveness.

Are you willing to consider conversations with difficult people as gifts? Without difficult people in our lives, we can't grow. Hard conversations and difficult people open the door to the potential for repair—which means *we* are the difficult people in need of restoration. A tricky interaction with a narcissistic, self-absorbed, self-righteous, hardheaded, hard-hearted person reveals our need to look to someone greater than ourselves; our longing to be free from the bondage of toxic negativity; our hope to invite others to their Storyteller of grace and forgiveness; and our need to forgive and be forgiven.

Mack, the main character in *The Shack*, asks Jesus, "Does that mean that all roads will lead to you?"

"Not at all," Jesus tells him. "Most roads don't lead any-where. What it does mean is that I will travel any road to find you."[26]

We can step out of the trap of fear to tell a deeper story than who is wrong, who is out, or who is unacceptable when we know—heart and soul—that there is never a conversation where God is not in the center of it *with us*. He doesn't watch and listen to our interactions from afar. He experiences them *with us*.

Trusting the Storyteller is in the story with us does not protect us from getting hurt. Being knocked down in a verbal sparring match can convince us that we are alone and being set up, sending us back into the unsafe haven of fear. But here is the truth: In the midst of fiery, tense, potentially vola-tile conversations, God chooses to identify *with us*. In that reality, every interaction is a gift—an opportunity to experience God's presence and a chance for personal transformation. He is in the story. And he's not leaving. Ever.

Begin Againers

We sat in Starbucks again, months after the sparring match between Jake and Haley. I spent the weeks in between these meetings thinking about my part in the conversation, beginning every morning and every evening meditating on the words of the Old Testament prophet Isaiah: "Don't panic. I'm with you. There's no need to fear for I'm your God. I'll give you strength. I'll help you. I'll hold you steady, keep a firm grip on you" (Isaiah 41:10). I also thought of the courageous declaration of three friends who stepped out of the trap of fear and engaged in a dangerous conversation long ago:

> Shadrach, Meshach, and Abednego told the difficult king, "We do not need to defend ourselves before you in this matter. If we are thrown into the blazing furnace, the God we serve is able to deliver us from it. . . . But even if he does not, we trust and know his love for us and will not trade our relationship with him for all the gold in your small kingdom."
> DANIEL 3:16-18, AUTHOR'S PARAPHRASE

I could feel God's steady grip on me and was ready for the furnace.

Haley started things off for this second go-around: "So, Jake, how are you feeling about our president now with the mess—the humanitarian crisis—we have at the border?"

Jake looked up from his cold-brew latte, and I caught his eye and entered the fray. "Jake, I've been thinking about the last time this subject came up. Where did you go when you left Starbucks?"

Jake looked surprised and a little embarrassed, but answered anyway. "I went to the bar. I guess I had enough fighting for one day."

"What do you mean?" I followed *his* story line.

"My wife and I are thinking about separating. That night she called me an arrogant jerk before I left for small group. When we all got together for coffee, I was still thinking about her words. I guess I just went ahead and proved she was right. I acted like a jerk. Haley, I'm sorry."

Haley stayed in the story and proved she wasn't as self-righteous as I judged her to be. "Jake, I'm sorry. Do you think we could all pray for you and your marriage?"

No fight. No furnace. We sat in Starbucks together— a group of raggedy hearts with and for one another. We belonged.

The twist in the conversation reminded me of an evening of babysitting years ago. The three children I was watching wanted to play a different version of hide-and-seek. In this version, everyone hides together while one person looks for the hidden. The seeker in our game was four-year-old Charlie. The rest of us hid in a discarded wardrobe dresser in a dark corner of the basement. We were crammed together, giggling and whispering, *"Shhh,"* as Charlie came down the stairs.

We heard his voice grow louder with each step down into the dark basement.

"I not afraid. I not afraid."

We froze in the wardrobe as Charlie got closer. The minute he started to open the door, we all jumped out and yelled, "Surprise!" And Charlie collapsed between us, exclaiming, "Everything I was looking for is right here!"

Charlie experienced common grace (in an uncommon way). What if everything we are looking for is in every interaction? Even with difficult people? Even if *we* are the difficult people? Without personal offense or paralyzing fear, we can *be* the change in the conversation.

(into action)

1. Take a week to detox from negativity. Call a friend and make a pact to avoid complaining for a week. Check in daily to share how it is going.

Consider these practices as part of your detox:

- When you caught yourself thinking about something in a negative way, how did you reframe your thoughts?

- When you were tempted to say something negative, did you believe your comments would add value to the conversation?
- When you saw someone through a negative lens, were you able to adjust to see something positive in that person?
- When you did say something negative, how did you rectify your remark?

2. Become a "begin againer" by praying, "*Lord, help me to Start Over today, with God's help from above. Give me the courage to approach all of this with the humility of a beginner. Every day. Openhanded and helpless.*"[27]

3. Mediate on Isaiah 41:10 and Daniel 3 morning and evening for a month.

4. Take out your jar of dust and broken pieces. Can you hear your Storyteller promising, "I'm in the center of it with you?"

5. Identify the difficult people in your life. Identify the difficult realities you contribute (rigid beliefs, a hard heart, unforgiveness). What keeps you from believing all you are hoping for can be found in your interactions with *those* people? What clues to how you can change the conversation can you find in your answer?

6. What do you want most? For the difficult people in your life to change or for transformation in your own life? If your longing is for personal transformation, get ready for an earthquake.

It is foolish to belittle one's neighbor;
    a sensible person keeps quiet.
PROVERBS 11:12, NLT

Your kindness will reward you,
    but your cruelty will destroy you.
PROVERBS 11:17, NLT

A gentle answer deflects anger,
    but harsh words make tempers flare.
PROVERBS 15:1, NLT

Gentle words are a tree of life;
    a deceitful tongue crushes the spirit.
PROVERBS 15:4, NLT

Wise words are like deep waters;
    wisdom flows from the wise like a
        bubbling brook.
PROVERBS 18:4, NLT

CHAPTER 7

Changing the Conversation

We can't get enough of each other if we can have each other at a digital distance—not too close, not too far, just right. But human relationships are rich, messy, and demanding. When we clean them up with technology, we move from conversation to the efficiencies of mere connection. I fear we forget the difference.
SHERRY TURKLE, *RECLAIMING CONVERSATION*

Real love stories don't have dictators, they have participants. Love is an ever-changing, complicated, choose-your-own adventure narrative that offers the world but guarantees nothing.
DONALD MILLER, *SCARY CLOSE*

I PROBABLY SHOULD NOT HAVE STARTED the conversation. I definitely should not have started it on Facebook, but I was having a day:

> I don't usually vent on FB. But today. Today a beautiful teenage girl with braces and impossible homework in math lays in a hospital bed after trying to end her life yesterday less than one hour after her school day ended. She's had boys (13-year-olds) say they just want to grab her body bc rape is good.

Other peers have mocked her for how she looks.
Still others have cruelly denigrated her with threats
that she doesn't belong. She's not welcome. She's an
outsider. No wonder the mental state of a teenager
today is similar to a psychiatric patient in the 1950s.
I'm angry. I'm angry at [leaders in our country who
have] publicly said and done the same things as
these middle school bullies. I'm sad that parents are
outsourcing parenting to schools and youth groups
and will defend their child's right to hurt a classmate
and deny them the grace of making an apology.

As I finished my post, my heart filled with longing for us
to change the conversation and stop tweeting taunts, justify-
ing objectification of women or men, and ripping away the
welcome mat from outsiders without the hint of an apology.
I longed to be part of a movement to be kind, because on
that day I knew it was a matter of life and death.

I knew I hinted at some potentially controversial subjects,
but I was not prepared for the comments posted in response
to my confession:

- Politics has nothing to do with this girl's mental
  illness.
- I'm unfriending you.
- God bless you, but I will have no part of what you are
  expressing.

- I don't see joy in you. I see hurt and anger and disappointment.
- You are perpetuating the hate in this country.
- Why are you ranting against our president?
- I don't think we need more laws to protect the gays from being mistreated, the blacks, the women, etc.
- Too many professing Christians seem to have a "me too" movement, a protest rally, and vagina hats as their vehicle to move past their experiences rather than God.

Wow! I hid my post after I read about half of the comments. How did what I thought was a plea for compassion and kindness turn into a relationally violent conversation about politics, sexuality, race, the Women's March, and my personal character? This one conversation quickly confirmed to me the provocative truth of journalist Colin Woodward's conclusion in his book *American Character*: Our country is more divided today than it has been since the Civil War.[1] I felt the war in the core of me. It rattled me to the bone.

The Cancer in Conversations

That day—more so than many—I was aware of the real consequences of conversations. When we are divided from each other, conversations become part of a pattern of disengagement rather than connection. Whether the dialogue is in the hallways of a middle school or on a social-media app, every conversation is potentially toxic and is likely to be marked by an opportunistic infection of division.

If we are looking to defend or condemn our politics, we can find a conversation that allows us to take sides. If we want to expose sexual harassment and abuse or affirm the work done in this area by many good organizations, we can find a conversation to affirm our place on the continuum. If we want to wage war, we can find reasons. If we want to march for peace, we will find allies. This is why *before* we engage in any conversation, we need to ask, "What am I looking for?" As I learned that day on Facebook, we do not live in times when we can impulsively post our perspective and not consider the consequences.

> **Groupthink:** *"Judging others makes us blind, whereas love is illuminating. By judging others we blind ourselves to our own evil and to the grace which others are just as entitled to as we are."*— *Bonhoeffer,* The Cost of Discipleship[2]

If we want our opinions to be puffed up, our perspectives to be "liked," our side to be winning, we can use conversation as a weapon in our divided world. The good news is that the opposite is also true. If we want to open the door to different opinions, to wrestle with our perspectives, and to connect with people no matter what side they are on, we can create conversations that offer a healing balm. But before we consider conversations as healing, we need to acknowledge why they have become so sick.

All of the division in our world has weakened our collective immune system. In the human body, every cell depends on the other cells. The New Testament likens a group of believers to an interconnected body: "So in Christ we, though many, form one body, and each member belongs to all the others" (Romans 12:5, NIV). When a group of cells joins together against the human body, cancer is the result. Could it be that when we join together against others, we create pain and death more than life?

I remember a client telling me about her first venture into a church service. Unbeknownst to her, the theme of the service was "the right to life." Two weeks earlier, she'd had an abortion. She was shaky, lonely, and confused when she walked into the church. The fervor and unity of the members of the congregation nudged her to slip out before she was even noticed.

Her story called to mind one of my own. A group of us met at a coffee shop to discuss a great book: *Made to Crave* by Lysa TerKeurst. Not one of us mentioned the woman sitting outside the coffee shop alone, smelling like alcohol and begging for spare change. While we discussed the book, sipping our lattes, I wondered if she was curious about this book on desire that we all carried into the coffee shop. Did we make her crave to belong to us? Did we even consider if she might want to be with us?

No matter how good our cause, when our conversations are tinged with even a hint of superiority, exclusivity, or self-righteousness, we weaken our collective immune system and become vulnerable to the cancer of division—potentially leaving others feeling attacked, left out, diminished, or even in peril. I can smell the fragrance of self-rightness and personal offense in my Facebook rant (the fact I recognize it as a rant is a clue that it was not intended to unite but to divide). I wince as I write that, because I believe I expressed some true and important ideas. But I want to be real. I need to be real and admit that the energy of the post was fueled by me and for me—to elevate me.

In order for healing to occur in the body, every cell must play its part of support. In order to address the cancer in our conversations, we need a serious change in how we view our interactions and the courage to be real before we can be supportive. We can't just vent on Facebook and not expect the consequences of a weakened immune system. Conversations are meant to be sacred, a conduit to reveal not only who we are but what we long for in the interaction: *love* (the opposite of elevating self).

Incremental change in our conversations is not enough. We need a complete overhaul. Changing the conversation requires us to take seriously the love story God is telling in us. Daily we must read our own lives and look for God's fingerprints of love on our stories, allowing our hearts to be penetrated and shaped by the love of God. As we do, common grace tells us that every conversation is an opportunity to reveal the vibrancy of God's love, and our conversations will be set ablaze—not with our being right but with our being loved.

When was the last time you had a vibrant conversation filled with all of the different textures, hues, and dimensions of God's love? We have the template: "We love because he first loved us" (1 John 4:19, NIV). When our hearts are imprinted with the template of God's adamant, unconditional love for us, love will be the primary story all our conversations are telling.

What would our world look like if our conversations were marked not by division but connection? Rachel Held Evans dared to "imagine if every church became a place where everyone is safe, but no one is comfortable."[3] Common grace allows people to be human, breathes life without prejudice, and knows—deeply knows—that we all suffer from the same condition. Grace sees another life in need of love. Not an "other" in need of love, but an image-bearer—one of us. We are pro-life when we are pro-grace for all people in all places.

We desperately need to change our conversations. The civil war in our country tells us that change may be a matter of life and death. When we experience—heart and soul—the vibrancy of God's love story in our stories, we *know* conversations are meant to take us together into the heart of God's story, because "Christianity isn't meant to simply be believed; it's meant to be lived, shared, eaten, spoken, and enacted in the presence of other people."[4] Changing the conversation from one of pain and death to one of life—bringing to our interactions "a vital fragrance, living and fresh" (2 Corinthians 2:16, AMPC)—is possible if we make bold choices to bring our belovedness into every conversation.

A Bold Choice about the Bible

The New Testament explains that the purpose of God's extravagant demonstration of love to us "is our peace, [for he] has made the two groups one and has destroyed the barrier, the dividing wall of hostility" (Ephesians 2:14, NIV). That's why most conversations infected by disconnection are incredibly painful: We are warring against each other and the purposes of God.

When we use the Bible in conversations to prove our superiority, justify our agenda, or make ourselves the judge of others, we create a dividing wall of hostility. Now, a difference in interpretation of the Bible, in and of itself, does not necessarily weaken the immune system of the collective body. Again, our human bodies are a metaphor for this reality. Every cell in our bodies has a cell wall, and those walls are open to other cells in order to sustain health throughout the body. We can change the conversation when we leave openings (doors) in our perspective—especially about the Bible. We open doors when we remember that while the Bible is inerrant, we are prone to errors of interpretation.

Argumentative: *to not care or try to understand the other person. Or even worse, to be determined to deliberately misunderstand and mischaracterize others, often to the point of absurdity.*

Is it possible for us to have diverse perspectives on the Bible without hostility? The Bible answers the question:

So making peace, Jesus "reconcile[s] both of them to God through the cross, by which he put to death their hostility" (Ephesians 2:16, NIV). The heart of God's story is peace. How many times have you heard a debate about the Scriptures and felt peace? Usually we leave aligning *with* one side and *against* another.

I am not suggesting that theology doesn't matter. It does. Theology is the study of the nature of God, and it is intended to remind us of the prize we are fighting for: people. The prize is to vibrantly love one another. A theology rooted in the story of the Cross is about making peace. It's about entering another person's story and calling it holy and staying *with* people, no matter what side they are on. A theology that creates healing conversations sticks close to the Door whenever someone starts to build a wall. Where is the Door? "Jesus told this simple story. . . . I am the Gate" (John 10:6, 9). When we are in the Door, we are in the one who is Love, "so we know and rely on the love God has for us. God is love. Whoever lives in love lives in God, and God in them" (1 John 4:16, NIV).

Most often, when we debate the Bible, we make secondary things primary. When we love our opinions, perspectives, or judgments at the expense of loving people, we are at risk of not loving people at all. C. S. Lewis put it like this: "Put first things first and we get second things thrown in: put second things first and we lose both first and second things. . . . You can't get second things by putting them first; you can get second things only by putting first things first."[5]

So what are "first things"? The apostle Paul answers this for us in his letter to new believers in Corinth:

> You'll remember, friends, that when I first came
> to you to let you in on God's sheer genius, I didn't
> try to impress you with polished speeches and the
> latest philosophy. I deliberately kept it plain and
> simple: first Jesus and who he is; then Jesus and what
> he did—Jesus crucified. . . . Your life of faith is a
> response to God's power, not to some fancy mental
> or emotional footwork by me or anyone else.
>
> 1 CORINTHIANS 2:1-5

In other words, as a Christian, my priority is not what I believe about politics, parenting, or other people. My highest calling is to camp out by the Door—to stay close to Jesus. That isn't evidenced by a quick sound bite on social media. Following Jesus is the messy, difficult, and heart-wrenching path of offering grace in every conversation.

How commited are we to killing hostility in conversations about things we are really, really passionate about . . . but are secondary to the love story of God? When we interact with others to prove and protect secondary things, we may experience a false sense of security. We are safe within walls that allow us to be the judge, but we remain far from the Door where starving people huddle, hungry for grace.

I think the lesson of "first things" is the message of Jesus to the woman who couldn't sit still because she was so busy getting it right. She was consumed with herself. She looked more competent and more in control than her sister, who lost herself at the feet of Jesus, hanging on his every word. Jesus reminded Martha—the one with the agenda, the woman of action, the one safe behind neat and tidy dividing lines—"Martha, Martha . . . you are worried and upset about many things, but few things are needed. . . . Mary has chosen [who] is better, and it will not be taken away from her" (Luke 10:41-42, NIV).

Let's be honest. We understand Martha. It's easier to get busy with secondary things and build walls of hostility than it is to adamantly and unashamedly love the one who is the Door to the way back to belonging to one another. Consider the cancer that grows when we build walls of hostility—especially in our theology:[6]

- If we believe someone has the "curse of Cain" (a terrible theology passionately debated 150 years ago to justify racism),[7] it's easier to make them our slaves.

- If we think someone is an inferior species (another theology millions died for during World War II), it's easier to exterminate them.

- If we use health and wealth to prove we are chosen (a popular televised theology), it's easier to keep our stuff in a world of poverty.

- If we are convinced some sins are worse than others (a theology that appeals to us all), it's easier to exclude the alcoholic, immigrant, and transvestite from lunch after church.

But if all other people (according to common grace) are reflections of the image of God, with the fingerprints of his love all over their stories, everything changes. That's the good news. What we *know* of the gospel can change our conversations—transforming them into conduits for Good News.

- **The gospel affects our posture in conversations.** Years ago I spoke for a retreat at the St. Malo retreat center in Allenspark, Colorado. (I even slept in the bed a former pope slept in while visiting Colorado years earlier!) One of the leaders from the center gave us a tour of the beautiful facility. In the Jesuit tradition, on almost every wall hung a crucifix. As we passed by one of those walls, the tour guide pointed at the vulnerable God, whose arms splayed open to all of us, and casually remarked, "That's a strange way to run the universe." Are our arms crossed, holding us apart from the world—or are they wide open to all?

- **The gospel orders our place in the conversation.** We think creating dividing walls will keep us safe, but maybe those walls enslave us by keeping us from others. I have a friend who started a ministry to the homeless in Denver. He's often asked to speak to groups about his ministry. He told me the question he's asked most is about numbers: *How many were saved?* He always answers the same: "Only one I know of: me. God is saving me through this work. I am the one who needs him most." His humble place in the story has opened the door (his ministry is actually called Open Door Ministries) to thousands of hurting people. Do we allow openings for others instead of jockeying for a place in the conversation?

- **The gospel compels us to use words in our conversations—only if necessary.** We need to be real. Are we afraid to engage with others—all others—without the so-called protection of a wall? A wall of words proclaiming our rightness, our proof, our position? Healing conversations begin when we tear down the wall and get close to all kinds of people. In his wonderful book *Scary Close*, Donald Miller writes, "Love doesn't control, and I suppose that's why it's the ultimate risk. In the end, we have to hope the person we're giving our heart to won't break it, and be willing to forgive them when they do, even as they will forgive us."[8] When we offer our hearts before we offer our opinion, words might not even be necessary. Offering our hearts means being willing to be vulnerable when we enter a conversation. Author and sociologist Brené Brown summarizes her definition of *vulnerability*:

Vulnerability is about showing up and being seen. It's waking up every day and loving someone who may or may not love us back, whose safety we can't ensure, who may stay in our lives or may leave without a moment's notice, who may be loyal to the day they die or betray us tomorrow. It's tough to do that when we're terrified about what people might see or think.[9]

- **Can we show up and be seen for who we really are for the sake of creating a space where others can belong, no matter who they are?**

A Bold Choice about Other People's Stories

Have you ever gone through an extraordinary experience or exhausting struggle or done something foolish or amazing and come to some powerful insights about yourself, others, and God? What happens if someone responds to your experience with doubt or dismissal? The Book of Wisdom in the Old Testament says, "Crushed hope makes the heart sick" (Proverbs 13:12, author's paraphrase). When someone denies our experience, not only our hope but our faith and love are crushed.

One of the most destructive choices we make is to join together to dismiss other people's stories. We most often are joined by our opinions, not a relationship. Joining in opinions opposes common grace, because the grace of God tells us that he would rather die than lose relationship with us. The one who was equal with God but made himself of no reputation so he could enter our stories shows us how to heal the conversation from the cancer of division: by simply being present in kindness (Philippians 2:6-7).

> **Dismissive:** *to brush aside or deprecate what others say instead of truly listening.*
>
> *One tip-off is "But . . ." But deletes whatever came before. "But a better way to look at it is . . ." Another tip-off is voice tone. If the response sounds irritated or deprecating, that's the sound of unwillingness to listen for what's valid in what is said.*

Why do we believe we need to be the judge of other people's stories and make our judgments known in conversations? Sometimes the answer is because we have not experienced the power of God's grace in our own stories. A few years ago, I was smack-dab in the middle of judging my daughter's story. She was irresponsible, making bad choices, and completely self-absorbed. I was about as far away from the Door as possible.

We were driving home after a late night out and her car started to sputter. I looked over at the dashboard of her fairly new car (that I helped her buy) and saw the flashing lights indicating that the radiator was about to blow. Sure enough, before I could get out the words "Why didn't you check the radiator fluid . . . ," steam spewed from the hood of the car, and we came to an abrupt stop. I was mad. I was right. My daughter's story was a tragedy of neglected responsibilities and missed opportunities. I had no intention of turning the conversation into something that might be life-giving to her.

We sat by the side of the road and I glanced at my watch. It was 12:30 a.m. Being skilled in the ways of martyr mothering, I called for an Uber to take my daughter home and said with an exasperated sigh, "I will take care of the car." I wasn't interested in my daughter's excuses or experiences. If I had been, I would have learned she didn't check the car because she had a health scare that kept her in the hospital most of the day to make sure her brain was not bleeding from an aneurysm doctors had found months earlier. I didn't ask. I gave up on her story while I waited for a tow truck.

I know now that it's impossible to give up on others' stories without giving up on our own. When I'm not curious about the struggle in someone else's life, I dismiss my own struggle. When I don't have faith that God is at work in another's story, I can't believe he is writing my own story. When I can't be with others in the midst of their messes, I don't hope God is with me in the midst of my messes. As the tow truck pulled away—leaving me in a Home Depot parking lot at 1:30 a.m.—God was still writing my story. Thank God he doesn't need our permission to keep writing our stories. But occasionally he gives us a glimpse of the splendor of his storytelling.

I noticed lights on across the road from Home Depot. It was a bar, and I quickly calculated I had thirty minutes before last call. When I dismissed my daughter's experience,

I was ready to sacrifice my own experience of sobriety on the altar of anger and self-pity. I crossed the street, anticipating the burn of alcohol going down my throat. I thought God would turn away from my story as quickly as I turned my back on my daughter's. I imagined he would stop watching me and leave me alone.

The bar was empty except for the two servers standing behind the counter. "What can I pour you?" A beautiful young woman, far too perky for 1:30 a.m., waited for my order. I was just about to ask for a sip of my forbidden fruit when I noticed a tattoo on her shoulder. I couldn't make out the words. Before I asked for a drink, I asked the bartender, "What does your tattoo say?"

"It's a Bible verse," she replied. A Bible verse? On a tattoo? In a bar at 1:30 in the morning, just as I'm about to throw away my story?

"It's from Psalms," this unlikely evangelist continued. "It's one of my favorite verses. It says, 'God is within her, she will not fall'" (Psalm 46:5, NIV). Can you believe that? The Grand Storyteller of my life showed up in a bar at 1:30 in the morning when my faith was tired, my hope seemed lost, and love was the last thing on my mind. I'd never read that verse before, but I knew God was writing it into my story just in the nick of time.

"So, what can I get you?" the bartender asked. I was already turning away, wandering back into my own story and ready to be with my daughter in hers. God graciously reminded me that he has set me free. He steadied me with his story so that I could be free to love as he loves and free to live beyond walls of hostility.

What's beyond the walls? A lot of really great stories.

We will not resolve most stories until redemption is complete in heaven, but we can participate in a communion of stories here on earth—if we don't dismiss other people's experiences. Dismissing another's story is taking away their words, consigning them to secrecy. The enemy of our stories loves secrecy, because when we dismiss another's experience, the cancer of disconnection metastasizes.

Astoundingly, one drop of grace can banish the cancer—even if it stings a little. Theologian Robert Capon reminds us of the grace that has been haunting us since the Garden:

> In the moment Adam and Eve eat of the fruit of
> the tree, they are redeemed. Not by that act but by
> him who made them. And therefore everything that
> happens after that is a proclamation of the gospel.
> . . . [God's grace] says, "Look, in your shape I
> wouldn't even think of letting you try to go back
> on your own. You cannot go back, you can only go
> forward into the mess you've made, but I will follow
> you every step of the way."[10]

God followed me into a bar and used a tattoo to show me that even though I was quick to dismiss my daughter's experience, he remained *with* me in mine. I couldn't wait to tell my daughter about the bartender, her tattoo, and the

Storyteller God who is within us, so we will not fall. God met me in my experience to reveal the scary, beautiful reality that we desperately need one another.

I love Anna McCarthy's blog about going with a group of pastors' wives to meet women who worked in strip clubs. Anna learned the power of *with* as she entered their stories:

> As I drove home, I totally fell apart in my car.
>
> Not because I felt sorry for them. Not because I thought I was so much better than they were. Not because I pitied their circumstance.
>
> I cried because my heart was broken.
>
> One thing the Lord continues to do in my heart is humble it. Like over and over. Countless times, I think I'm going in to minister to some lowly soul and then I walk out, completely undone because the condition of my own heart was exposed. . . .
>
> Man. HE WRECKED ME.
>
> [I learned,] "Apparently other churches send [these women] hate mail. ALL THE TIME." . . .
>
> Did we forget (or do we just sing it in songs) that Jesus was a friend of sinners?
>
> Did we forget that it's his kindness that leads us to repentance? . . .
>
> Jesus was UNAFRAID of walking in love to the least of the least. . . .
>
> . . . if Jesus were here, walking among us, wouldn't it be just like him to walk into the most

un-Christlike place (strip club or whatever) and completely freak the religious folk out?

Just a thought.

He loved then.

He loves now.

But, he can only reach as far as you and I are willing to go.[11]

What stories are you willing to walk into? What makes the gospel Good News isn't who it excludes but who it pursues. The night Jesus walked into my story when I was in a bar at 1:30 in the morning, I decided to stop debating other people's experiences and trust God to be the Storyteller. Author Dallas Willard, known for his writings on spiritual formation, explains it this way: "We don't believe something by merely saying we believe it, or even when we believe that we believe it. We believe something when we act as if it were true."[12]

God graciously allowed me to experience the power of *with* about six months later when my daughter posted this on Facebook. As I reread it now, I am humbled and grateful that God keeps writing our stories. He uses Facebook, politics, teenagers, presidents, coffee shops, mental illness, Christian books, addiction, bars, broken radiators, health struggles, tattoos, strip clubs, and you and me. He uses everything and doesn't waste anything. Oh, for grace to love like him!

Through my experiences in activism, I've noticed
that I get the most push-back from people who also
use the name of Jesus or a personal interpretation of
the Bible adapted to fit today's politics. It has been
harmful to me on several occasions. . . .

While my political beliefs may not align with
my mom's (and are even on opposing ends on some
issues), my mom has creatively sought out [ways to]
connect with me on "my" level.

As a result, I've accepted her invite to [church]
this Sunday evening. . . . It's softened my heart . . .
there are still people like my . . . mother who care
enough to speak the language of Love.[13]

Don't think that God is done writing this part of my story,
or that his grace is unique to me. If Jesus will go to the end
of the world and hang on a cross to get one self-absorbed,
recovering alcoholic who can be a pinched and paltry mom—
he will go to anyone, anywhere. You see, I am really the
image-bearer of God—loved before the foundation of the
world, brought into a deeper story of beloved belonging and
allowed to invite others into that story as well. Choosing to be
with my daughter in her story opened the door to decisions
to be with others I never imagined would be part of my life.
It turns out that the truth God showed me after walking into
a bar is the Door to *way More*. When I stopped debating the
Bible and dismissing others' experiences, my conversations

started to change, and God stretched his tent for me to be with people way outside my comfort zone.

Where is the Story taking you? The Kingdom of God is for liars, outcasts, addicts, oddballs, fools, and the totally uncool gathered in a communion of stories because they are hungry for *More*.[14]

Go. Invite everyone. Whisper or shout, "'Welcome! There's bread and wine. Come eat with us and talk.' This isn't a kingdom for the worthy; it's a kingdom for the hungry.[15] You belong!"

(into action)

1. Write your own translation of 1 Corinthians 13 (God's medicine for healing conversations). Here is mine:

> If I speak with the words of certainty, power, and control but don't love my wayward children, the powerless addict, and my falling-down fellow travelers, I'm nothing but the creaking of a rusty gate.
>
> If I write and speak God's Word to those who believe and think like me, but I don't talk about him to those I don't understand or agree with, I'm nothing.

If I give everything I own to a great cause and don't join in vulnerably with others—allowing them to really see me—I've gotten nowhere.

So, no matter what I say, what I believe, and what I do, I'm bankrupt without love that finds a way back for us to belong to one another.

2. Create a pattern for the word *with*. It can be on paper or in clay, stamped on metal or communicated through any medium you can imagine. Get ready for your jar of dust and broken pieces to be transformed.

I learned that faith isn't about knowing all of the right stuff or obeying a list of rules. It's something more, something more costly because it involves being present and making a sacrifice. Perhaps that's why Jesus is sometimes called Immanuel—"God with us." I think that's what God had in mind, for Jesus to be present, to just be with us. It's also what He has in mind for us when it comes to other people.

The world can make you think that love can be picked up at a garage sale or enveloped in a Hallmark card. But the kind of love that God created and demonstrated is a costly one

because it involves sacrifice and presence.
. . . It's a brand of love that doesn't just think
about good things, or agree with them, or talk
about them. . . . [It's] the simple truth that
continues to weave itself into the tapestry of
every great story:

Love does.

BOB GOFF[16]

(transforming grace)

PART III

We draw people to Christ not by loudly discrediting what they believe, by telling them how wrong they are and how right we are, but by showing them a light that is so lovely that they want with all their hearts to know the source of it.

MADELEINE L'ENGLE, *WALKING ON WATER*

Transformed people transform people.

RICHARD ROHR, *EAGER TO LOVE*

CHAPTER 8

Changing the Cast of Characters

The natural impulse in life is to move upward, to grow in wealth, power, success, standing. And yet all around the world you see people going downward. We don't often use the word "humbling" as a verb, but we should. All around the world there are people out there humbling for God. They are making themselves servants. They are on their knees, washing the feet of the needy, so to speak, putting themselves in situations where they are not the center; the invisible and the marginalized are at the center. They are offering forgiveness when it makes no sense, practicing a radical kindness that takes your breath away.

DAVID BROOKS, *THE SECOND MOUNTAIN*

IT WAS MY FATHER'S EIGHTY-FIFTH BIRTHDAY. My brother and I arrived early and set up the tables and chairs. We worked efficiently. We tied a few balloons to a lamppost in front of the retirement community center and Presto! Change-o! We were ready to get this show on the road. The caterers set up all the fixings for a barbecue-palooza, and I started to wait (rather impatiently) for the guests to arrive. For Christmas, I offered my dad the party as a gift—suggesting he invite a few close friends and family members. I should have expected my parents' response to my gift, but I was caught off guard when they posted the invitation in their *church bulletin*. Rather than getting ready for a dozen or so guests, we set up the party for almost forty people!

My parents' church is a small congregation of about fifty members. It's a community church named Grace. My parents, in their eighties, are some of the youngest congregants. Their church doesn't have a worship band. In fact, when my dad was eighty-two years old, he and another elder climbed into the attic to turn the volume on the organ down. They didn't want to dim the joy of the ninety-year-old organist by asking her to play a little quieter. The members of this church don't always remember to turn on their hearing aids or bring their reading glasses. They don't walk quickly. In fact, they don't do anything fast—and that is outside my comfort zone of speed, efficiency, and competency.

I found myself checking the front door of the community center for the geriatric set to arrive and tapping my foot a little impatiently. You'd think I would know from my foot-tapping experience at Einstein Bros. Bagels that I was merely alerting the Storyteller of my life by my impatient antics that I needed more content written into my story—and maybe more characters.

Slowly, the elderly members of my parents' church made it to the party. Nearly the last to arrive was Mary Ann. Her gnarled hands gripped her walker as she haltingly made her way toward me. I doubt Mary Ann watches *Game of Thrones* or spends much time talking about the politics of the day, but she knows everything about my adult children and tells my parents every week that she is still praying for us all. She is known for the literal calluses on her knees.

"Mary Ann!" I greeted her. "I am so glad you could make it."

"How are your children, dear Sharon?" she asked. My heart settled in the peace she exudes. I told her they are doing well and thanked her for praying.

"Oh, that isn't hard," she said with a twinkle in her bright-blue eyes. "I don't have anything better to do."

I knew she meant it.

I thanked God for introducing me to this cast of characters from my parents' church and prayed he would slow me down to learn the wisdom of those who don't have anything "better" to do. The gracious Storyteller introduced new characters to my story—not so much for what I could offer them, but for what they could offer me. Every new character who walks into my story is potentially an agent of change, but this is where things can get tricky.

New characters can be controversial. Most are not as easy to love as Mary Ann. Including new characters in our stories can make us suspect. There is a reason why we marginalize people to the edges of our lives. Evil's commitment is to make our stories and their cast of characters small. Evil's primary directive is to convince us to *not* give our presence to others or receive theirs.

> **Marginalization:** *"treatment of a person, group, or concept as insignificant or peripheral."*[1]

The elderly are only one segment of our society who are often invisible—even, and perhaps especially, in the church. Absorbed in that invisibility are the experiences, losses, hopes, and fears of years of stories. One author describes this often-left-out cast of characters:

> There's a quiet generation of people who are
> being blatantly shunned and abused. They are the
> "invisible" generation; the elderly among us who
> are often regarded as feeble-minded and lacking in
> the ability to contribute to society in a meaningful
> way. This ageist attitude has robbed senior citizens
> of their self-worth, leaving them the victims of
> prejudice and disrespect. Compassion, courtesy, and
> respect have gone by the wayside.[2]

Sadly, our culture has marginalized women like Mary Ann, and the result is that we are stories who are anemic, desperate for the rich lifeblood that comes from the stories of other image-bearers.

When I am the most important character in my story, I miss the characters who might be the catalysts to transforming grace in my life. If common grace is recognizing the image of God in everyone and considering every conversation as potentially life-giving, then transforming grace lives on the edges—outside of what is perceived by our culture as "acceptable." When the cast of characters in our stories is determined by who makes us look good, who agrees with us, who elevates us, or who makes us comfortable, our stories become much smaller than God intended. Daring to go outside our "bubble" of conformity to invite in those on the margins creates a metamorphosis of belonging.

As I began to experience the story of love God is writing in me—a story that stretched me to love my daughter (even and especially because she is different from me)—I started to wonder what other characters I might be missing. It really wasn't hard to learn to speak my daughter's language or to invite Mary Ann into my life. Love for both of them came naturally—and, quite honestly, is acceptable and often expected by our culture. But what about love for the more marginalized? People of different lifestyle choices, ethnicities, or belief systems who are outside the walls of familiarity and acceptability?

Stretching the Tent

Real transformation began to shake in the depths of my being when I recognized that God actually gives us a cue, an alert signal that he is at work stretching our hearts and our stories. Surprisingly, the warning signal is shame. Like the proverbial red light on the dashboard of a car, shame tells me that something needs to be done—but I know I'm not the one with any skills or training to do anything about it.

Shame signals that something is not well in our hearts, and we don't know how to fix it. I felt the flicker of that light when I started tapping my foot impatiently, waiting for my father's party guests to arrive. Shame reveals an ugly or unlovely part of our souls.

For most of us, shame—not the purposes of God—shapes the cast of characters in our stories. We avoid the man living in sexual sin, the teenager who chooses the Wiccan religion, the family whose ethnic beliefs and customs we don't understand, because it helps us escape shame—the sense that something is unfamiliar to us and we aren't competent to deal with it.

We violate love when we avoid people because we don't know what to say or do and don't believe that interacting with people at the edges of our lives might introduce us to beauty, goodness, and gratitude. Fear and pressure are what energize us—we think we will be exposed as fools for loving someone suspect, as unwise for inviting people who make bad choices to eat dinner with us, as naive for not knowing the right words. And so we invite our cast of characters on the basis of what is acceptable or familiar instead of what is sacred.

Prejudice: *"preconceived opinion that is not based on reason or actual experience."*[3]

The power of shame is that it makes us small. It silences us. Because we don't want to feel stupid, suspect, judged, or incompetent, we avoid other image-bearers who aren't like us. We become a part of a faceless mob who all look alike, talk alike, believe alike, and, sadly, exclude alike. All this exclusivity is eased by our technology. We can write someone off and never look that person in the eye. We can condemn a whole group of people and not ever see a single face.

Our face shows our unique identity. It is who we are. Our face reveals more of who we are made to be than any other part of us. When we risk expanding our stories to include a more diverse cast of characters, *we* are transformed when we come face-to-face with others. Inviting others into my story—even when I know all is not well and I don't know how to fix things—shakes my heart and soul into the realm of transforming grace.

We may talk and think about grace a lot, but that isn't enough. Grace needs to be the theme of our stories—the very air we breathe, the relationships we include, the transla-tion of our experience with Jesus to others. Grace isn't just a theologically interesting category. *It's how we live and who we live with.*

If we're going to stretch the tent to add others to our stories, we need to be honest enough about our need for Jesus that we can call our judgment, fear, people-pleasing, disdain, and exclusion of others *sin*. Only when our under-standing of our sin confronts us with our constant need for forgiveness can we be ushered into transforming grace.

I'm speaking about myself here: I have used theological constructs and cultural norms as justification for turning away others because I don't want to admit how afraid I am of differences. I don't want others to see how critical I can be. I don't want you to know how petty and mean I am, so I have learned to hide under a cloak of acceptability while the cancer of division metastasizes. And I suspect I'm not alone.

We don't stretch the tent because we submit to a framework of rules constructed out of fear of man, not fear of God. We fear if we're not with others in the correct political party, on the right side of certain issues, or on the right side of lifestyle choices, we will miss out on the inner sanctum of acceptability. But, as Mark Labberton notes, "Ordinary, daily acts of prejudice, hatred, disdain, neglect, indifference, and self-absorption [reveal] that, if we have received grace, we have hoarded it. . . . We cannot hoard without something in or around us rotting. We proclaim a gospel that transforms."[4]

Transforming grace takes us into the margins, where we no longer compromise love to be part of the inner ring and we cast off the cloak of acceptability. A pleasing facade is not good news. The Good News is that the rightness of Christ is our clothing and he invites us to wear him wherever we go, whoever we're *with*. His covering empowers us for *withness*. Our own transformation compels us to invite others to know the story of love God is writing in our lives, and in the process, God keeps writing the story—keeping us out of the fetid place of exclusion and taking us into the flourishing place of inclusion.

The apostle Paul describes what this transforming grace looks like:

Because of this decision we don't evaluate people
by what they have or how they look. We looked at

the Messiah that way once and got it all wrong, as you know. We certainly don't look at him that way anymore. Now we look inside, and what we see is . . . the old life is gone; a new life emerges! Look at it! All this comes from the God who settled the relationship between us and him, and then called us to settle our relationships with each other. God put the world square with himself through the Messiah, giving the world a fresh start by offering forgiveness of sins. God has given us the task of telling everyone what he is doing. We're Christ's representatives. God uses us to persuade men and women to drop their differences and enter into God's work of making things right between them. We're speaking for Christ himself now: Become friends with God; he's already a friend with you.

2 CORINTHIANS 5:16-20

The invitation to become friends with God is not limited to *me*. It's for *all of us*. So yes, God is my friend. But is he also a friend of the bisexual? The Muslim? The opiate addict? Yes, yes, yes.

Let me get a little more personal. God is a friend to the frustrated black school teacher who highlights my inadequacy in understanding his world, and God wants me to be a friend to him too. God is a friend to the woman who paints my nails and makes an offering to her Buddhist idol every day, and he wants me to be a friend to her too. God is a friend to the same-sex-attracted woman who sits quietly in the back row of church and slips out before we all take Communion because she's not sure she's welcome, and he wants me to be a friend to her too. God is a friend to the rescued sex worker who is considering going back on the job because her dad is sick and they don't have health insurance or health care of any kind in her country—and he wants me to be a friend to her too.

In his book *The Second Mountain*, columnist and best-selling author David Brooks describes having reached an enviable summit of success and acclaim. When his twenty-seven-year marriage ended in divorce and depression overwhelmed him, he realized he needed to climb a second mountain—one that offered meaning through an expanded community. A friend told him, "I've never seen a program turn around a life. Only relationships turn around lives."[5] David Brooks began exploring a second mountain, one in which ascent begins with apparent descent into relationships he never considered before. Descent and ascent into the transforming grace of relationships has also changed my story in profound and unshakable ways—leading me down unexpected and beautiful paths toward belonging.

All My Stories Are White

Occasionally, I have the privilege of speaking for the National Center for Youth Issues, an organization providing in-service training on values education for public-school teachers. I was invited to speak at a middle school in a suburb of Nashville,

Tennessee. I did not research my audience, and so I was a bit shaken when I walked into a room of all African American teachers. I sensed a red light flashing on the dashboard of my heart, but I ignored it and welcomed everyone cheerfully. "I'm so grateful we get to spend this day together."

"The whole day?" One younger teacher, with a baseball cap on backward, groaned. The principal glared at him, and the man looked at the floor. I plowed ahead into my standard presentation. I started with some statistics about middle schoolers, told a story of one of my thirteen-year-old clients, and played a song about teenage angst.

One brave teacher raised her hand and asked me if I knew the rap version of the song. I quickly answered, "No," and kept talking. The warning light was starting to make me literally shake as I saw I was losing my audience, but I didn't know what to do. Shame stalked at the corner of the room, threatening to shrink, silence, and shape me.

Thank God, his Spirit is more powerful than shame. The Author who wrote, "The Holy Spirit, God's gift, does not want you to be afraid of people, but to be wise and strong, and to love them and enjoy being with them" (2 Timothy 1:7, TLB), was writing dialogue into my story, inviting some new characters into its cast.

After about fifteen minutes of bumbling into my presentation, I stopped. I turned off the PowerPoint, closed my notebook, and acknowledged, "I don't know what I'm doing here. You probably figured that out. All of my stories are white. My music is white. I don't know much about your world at all. I do know you are in the trenches. You are these kids' parents, grandparents, counselors, doctors, coaches, chauffeurs, nutritionists, and teachers. Maybe we can learn something from each other if we just talk."

White privilege: *"White privilege is both unconsciously enjoyed and consciously perpetuated. It is both on the surface and deeply embedded into American life. It is a weightless knapsack—and a weapon.*

It depends on who's carrying it."[6]

The room let out a collective sigh as these unsung heroes started to tell me their stories of feeling left behind in the era of "no school left behind." We brainstormed about resiliency and ideas for talking about values in a world where groceries, health care, and overwhelmed parents are priorities. At the end of the day, I thanked the group for teaching me about their world and asked if anyone had anything they wanted to add to the conversation. The man who groaned at the beginning of the day raised his hand. His name is John, and he teaches math and home economics as well as coaching football. I will never forget his request: "Will you pray for us?" I looked at the principal for permission, and she nodded her head.

Before I could pray, another man asked if he could pray too. I fumbled through a prayer, knowing I was on the sacred ground of communal stories of suffering and persevering. My limited experience with diverse communities and my prejudice (oh, how I wince as I write that!) did not prepare me for his prayer. He explained after he prayed that he was reading a book on prayer by Walter Brueggemann and had found a prayer (probably while I was babbling on) that he thought applied to our day. I can still hear his gravelly voice, tinged by a Southern accent:

> *When the world spins crazy,*
>   *spins wild and out of control*
>   *spins toward rage and hate and violence . . .*
> *And when we meet you hiddenly,*
>   *we find the spin not so unnerving,*
>   *because from you the world again has a chance*
>   *for life and sense and wholeness.*
> *We pray midst the spinning, not yet unnerved,*
>   *but waiting and watching and listening,*
>   *for you are the truth that contains all our spin. Amen.*[7]

I email back and forth with the principal and both of these teachers, who are still at the school. Their suffering-and-still-hanging-in-there examples are transformative in my days of suffering and looking for hope. David Brooks's words capture who these new characters have been in my story:

> "[Their suffering has] a way of exposing the deepest parts of ourselves and reminding us that we're not the people we thought we were. People in the valley have been broken open. They have been reminded

that they are not just the part of themselves that they put on display."[8]

I know I have so much to learn about racial tension and unity and that most of my experiences and stories (and songs) are still white, but I am so grateful for those who are willing to put up with me and share their own stories. I am motivated to stretch the tent of my story by the words of Jim Wallis, editor in chief of *Sojourners*: "Confronting the barriers of race, class, culture, and gender was perhaps the major social drama of the New Testament church. Overcoming these divisions was seen as a primary test of spiritual authenticity."[9]

Spiritual authenticity—and the characters who introduce us to it—is a gift of transforming grace.

Red Nails and Buddha

I have the best manicurist in the city. Her name is Annie, and I send all my friends to her for their manicures and pedicures. I told my friend Sharla about her, and she became a regular customer. I also told Sharla that I watch with sadness sometimes when I'm waiting for Annie in the nail salon. I've watched her carry a plate with a pyramid of shiny red apples and kneel down to place them carefully on the floor before a fat ceramic Buddha painted with red garments (a shade darker than my favorite nail color). I feel sad as I see Annie kneel before a god who looks at her with eyes that cannot see over the bounty of apples it cannot taste.

Not too long ago, I came into the salon, and Annie

greeted me with a big smile. "Look!" She pointed to a beautiful bouquet of flowers and laughed. "Sharla brought them to me. Just because!" I called Sharla later to tell her about Annie's joy over the flowers. Sharla explained she brought them to Annie "because I want her to know she's more than a manicurist to me. I want her to know I care about her. I want to tell her about Jesus."

Sharla's generosity challenged me. Mark Labberton expands on why:

> This is the shock of Jesus' call to his disciples. [Jesus] was always seeing people differently from how his disciples did. He stopped to see those who could have been ignored. He remembered, in age, lifestyle, circumstances, spiritual condition, those on whom many around him closed the shutters. Jesus relentlessly opens the shutters. . . . This act of [transformation] is . . . evidence that our shuttered windows are now open and opening wider still.[10]

Bearing witness: *a sense of togetherness that is honored with mutual respect, creating courage to share our stories and hope that we can anticipate more to come.*

Sharla was inviting me to open the shutters and add Annie to my story—not as a faceless walk-on but as a significant character in the story. Sharla and I have begun to pray for chances to tell Annie about the love story of Jesus. We are scheduling more frequent manicures.

Along the way, God is challenging me about my own attempts to bargain with him, reminding me I'm not all that different from Annie. I catch myself wondering, *If I read my Bible every day, will God rescue my children? If I don't drink, smoke, or swear too much, will he bless my counseling practice? If I eat my vegetables (at least once a day), will he preserve my health and lower my cholesterol?* I don't offer fruit to a lifeless statute, but I offer control, trying harder, and being better to the one who was crucified and rose from the dead so that I would never worship something that's not even worth it.

When you see a nail salon, will you pray for Annie and Sharla and me? We are trusting in the God who sees us, and no matter what we offer, we know he only sees Love.

Transforming grace keeps the shutters open, eagerly welcoming new cast members, asking God for the courage to see and be seen and the vision to perceive the needs of people as he does. And sometimes it brings flowers just because.

Communion in the Midst of Sexual Confusion

Janie goes to my church. She used to sit in the back row and would always leave before Communion because she wasn't sure she should join us. She is asking questions about her sexuality and acknowledges she is attracted to women, but doesn't want to act out of her confusion. She also reads her Bible, asks good questions, and loves Jesus. She longs to talk about all of this in community but doesn't know how. She confessed these feelings to me one Sunday night after church, and I could feel the warning light going off again. I didn't know what to say. I knew there was something about Janie's confession that seemed right, but I feared if I got involved, it could go terribly wrong.

I am studying to teach a class on sexuality and just read *Sexual Ethics: An Evangelical Perspective* by Stanley Grenz, who suggests sexuality is broader than sex. He writes, "This drive to bond with others in community is an expression of our fundamental sexuality, a sexuality that goes deeper than body parts, potential roles in reproduction, and genital acts."[11] Reducing Janie to her same-sex attraction dismissed her holy longing for community and made me an active participant in distorting her sexuality.

I winced as I thought about Janie's "drive to bond with others in community" being unmet in the empty back row of the church. One Sunday night, as Communion was about to begin, I thought about what Jesus would do with Janie. I could not imagine him letting her slip out of the church alone, so I went to the front of the church and took two pieces of bread and two little Communion cups of wine and went to find Janie. She had already exited the church. I followed after her, half-running while trying not to spill the wine on the sidewalk. "Janie!" I called out. She stopped and stared at me. I know I looked a little crazed, out of breath, trying to balance the bread and the wine.

"Janie, I just want you to share this with me. It represents Christ's body, broken for you." I handed her a piece of the bread. After we both finished chewing the bread, Janie surprised me and took both cups of the wine from me. She pushed one cup toward me while her eyes filled with tears: "And this is Christ's blood shed for you." We both drank our Communion cup and then looked at each other. After a few minutes, Janie smiled and said, "Thank you. I'll see you next week." She does come every week, and she doesn't slip out before Communion anymore.

> **Mutuality:** *"A community identifies itself by an understood mutuality of interests. But it lives and acts by the common virtues of trust, goodwill, forbearance, self-restraint, compassion, and forgiveness. If it hopes to continue long as a community, it will wish to—and will have to—encourage respect for all its members, human and natural. It will encourage respect for all stations and occupations. Such a community has the power—not invariably but as a rule—to enforce decency without litigation. It has the power, that is, to influence behavior. And it exercises this power not by coercion or violence but by . . . preserving stories and songs."*[12]

I am certain there are some who will have theological arguments with my actions. This is partly why I wrote this book. If a few more people feel welcomed to talk about their struggles in the church, then I will rejoice. My experience, as a therapist, has taught me that when people are moved to the margins because they struggle with sexuality, addiction, abuse, or broken relationships, they are much more likely to align with those outside the church. After all, souls are connected in pain. When we can talk openly within the church, we are all called to holiness and sacrifice. Sharing my Communion with Janie was a holy sacrifice. It is clear to me that we cannot deal with old problems in the same old ways. It's not working. I hope the new way is love that casts out fear, unbuckles assumptions, and finds every struggle and conversation about it as the context to reveal the brilliance of the gospel—Christ's body broken and blood shed for all of us.

I am grateful for Janie. She compelled me to confront my cowardice. I recently read that Henri Nouwen, who was called to celibacy, believed people with same-sex attraction serve a unique purpose in the Christian community. He endorsed Carl Jung's view that "[gay] people are often endowed with an abundance of religious feelings, and a spiritual receptivity that makes them responsive to revela-tion."[13] Janie's courage to confess an unpopular struggle and stay in community is a revelation to us all. She demonstrates the poignant truth described by theologian Ronald Rolheiser: "Our hearts, minds, and souls are Grand Canyons without a bottom. Because of that we will, this side of eternity, always be lonely, restless, incomplete . . . living in the torment of the insufficiency of everything attainable."[14]

Relationally, we are ultimately unfillable. Rather than be afraid of Janie's controversial struggle, I am convicted to look at my own ways of trying to control my holy hunger—even if it's from morsels of people-pleasing. I am so glad Janie is in my life, a part of my communion of desire.

Transforming grace relentlessly reveals to me that Jesus is

the love I have been looking for all of my life—and that he never stops looking for me, even when I want to sneak out the door before anyone sees me. And that compels me to look for other sneaky characters to add to my story.

Missionary Madness

After walking some dark days together, my daughter and I decided to get busy living. We traveled to Cambodia for almost a month to be with young women rescued from the horrors of sex trafficking. When we first arrived, we were overwhelmed with the heat, mosquitoes, strange smells, and even stranger foods. We met the young women the first day we arrived. I could claim I was suffering from jet lag, but really, I was suffering from ignorance and what I call "missionary madness."

The local missionaries suggested we play a few games to get to know the young women. Now mind you, we didn't speak the language. My bright idea was to play the game that begins with, "I'm going on a trip, and I'm taking . . ." Each person suggests an item they are bringing and then every person in the circle adds their item, remembering the items already chosen. This is a challenging game when everyone speaks the same language. It cannot be called anything but madness to suggest this game to a group that does not share a common tongue. Everyone tried to play along until we all collapsed in the ruins of not understanding the game, not understanding each other, and certainly not understanding why I was the leader of anything!

That night, as we were going to bed, I turned to my

daughter and admitted, "I don't know if I can do this!" Before we left the women's center, I learned that one of the girls was thinking about going back into the sex-worker business to provide income for her desperate family. It all felt hopeless. I forgot that the red, flashing light throbbing inside of me was an alert that God was writing more of my story. Kristin reminded me, "Mom, you don't have a choice. We still have nineteen days left!"

The next day, after a restless sleep during which I imagined all kinds of insects crawling into my bed, I greeted the morning with halfhearted determination. This was hard. I didn't stop to think how hard this was for these young women every day. Kristin reminded me to use the bottled water to brush my teeth, and I started to cry.

When we got to the living quarters for the women, we sensed that a party was about to start. I couldn't imagine a party in this setting. Most of the women did not even have shoes. What kind of party would we have? Kristin and I sat down in the meeting room, and one by one, every young woman marched by us and presented *us* with gifts—pictures of their families, flowers picked from the yard, origami creatures they had folded together carefully, nail polish! I wasn't sure where the nail polish came from but learned later that one of the trades the women's center taught to the women was that of a nail technician.

I was speechless at the generosity of these new characters in my story. While I sat dazed by jet lag, culture shock, and my own raggedy heart, Kristin sat down on the floor in the middle of the women, and they started painting one another's nails. A collage of images crowded my mind—the years of Kristin struggling just to live, of the two of us fighting to love each other, of our determination to stay in the story. Today as I reflect on this story, I think of something David Brooks wrote: "The season of suffering interrupts the superficial flow of everyday life. They see deeper into themselves and realize that down in the substrate, flowing from all the tender places, there is a fundamental ability to care, a yearning to transcend the self and care for others. And when they have encountered this yearning, they are ready to become a whole person."[15]

Oh, and the young woman so desperate to help her family that she was about to quit on her story and return to the dark treachery of sex trafficking? Her name means *moonlight*. She and Kristin became friends. They stay in touch (through the mission we traveled with), and Kristin organized a support campaign for her with her friends and a few local churches. Often, when we see the moon, we think of this young woman and entrust her to the one who created the moon to pull an entire ocean from shore to shore and created a circle of belonging between two young women on opposite sides of the world.

Transforming grace makes us ready to transform our yearnings into caring for others and transcending ourselves to find a way to new characters in our stories—even on the other side of the world.

Does this belonging to one another sound too good to be true? There is no doubt the way back includes sacrificing our safety, our sense of comfort, our biases and fears, in pursuit of someone who may be outside the "seat" we're used to sitting in. Adding characters to the wayback could make it crowded, uncomfortable, and even a little more dangerous. The question we need to end with is *Do we want to store our stories in the world we see, or in the world that is unseen, the world that is too good to be true?* We will find the unseen world coming into focus as we change the cast of characters in our stories. Or, as the New Testament suggests, "We don't look at the troubles we can see now; rather, we fix our gaze on things that cannot be seen. For the things we see now will soon be gone, but the things we cannot see will last forever" (2 Corinthians 4:18, NLT).

I don't know about you, but I want to be part of a story that will last forever.

(into action)

1. Have you ever felt invisible? If you pay attention to your vulnerabilities and to the work of God within you, what does the feeling of invisibility tell you that you need from others?

2. Who are the people at the edges of your life? Why are they there? How can you be *with* them?

3. Tell your own stories of being surprised at what happened when you stretched the tent of your story

to include others. What did they offer you? What
new truths did God write in your story?

4. How can you be more authentic?

5. How do you measure your worth or the worth of
   others?

6. Is there anyone you are afraid to be in a relationship
   with? Why?

7. Take pieces from your jar of dust and glass, and glue
   it into the pattern of *with* you created earlier.

8. When you think of the cast of characters in your
   story right now, who is missing? What do you find
   yourself most longing for? God sees us. He hears us.
   He understands us. Tell him who you are missing.
   Tell him what you long for. He longs to be with us.
   It's a promise: "I will be with you always, even until
   the end of the world" (Matthew 28:20, CEV).

> I saw Holy Jerusalem, new-created,
> descending resplendent out of Heaven, as
> ready for God as a bride for her husband.
>   I heard a voice thunder from the Throne:
> "Look! Look! God has moved into the
> neighborhood, making his home with men
> and women! They're his people, he's their
> God. He'll wipe every tear from their eyes.

Death is gone for good—tears gone, crying gone, pain gone. . . . Look! I'm making everything new. . . ."

Then he said, "It's happened. I'm A to Z. I'm the Beginning, I'm the Conclusion. From Water-of-Life Well I give freely to the thirsty. . . . I'll be God to them, they'll be sons and daughters to me."

REVELATION 21:2-7

(unexpected grace)

PART IV

*Grace is the celebration of life, relentlessly
hounding all the non-celebrants in
the world. It is a floating, cosmic bash
shouting its way through the streets of
the universe, flinging the sweetness of its
cassations to every window, pounding at
every door in a hilarity beyond all liking
and happening.*

ROBERT FARRAR CAPON, *BETWEEN
NOON AND THREE*

*God makes the world not out of necessity
but by a divine Whim, and the world he
makes is a whimsically romantic place.
We're all crazy for each other because
we're made in the image of Someone who's
always been crazy about us.*

ROBERT FARRAR CAPON, *GENESIS: THE
MOVIE*

CHAPTER 9

Every Moment

The best criticism of the bad is
the practice of the better.
RICHARD ROHR, TWITTER

THE SETTING COULD NOT BE MORE FAMILIAR TO ME. The cast of characters, although always changing, somehow remains constant in reminding me of Home. The conversation always starts the same: "My name is Sharon, and I'm an alcoholic."

On this day I sat in the familiar circle of chairs in the musty church basement, smelling of Sunday school and coffee, to celebrate ten years of sobriety. Although recovery has been a part of my life for thirty years, my three-steps-forward and two-steps-back journey brought me to ten years of sobriety in February 2019. Following the traditions of our meeting, I received a celebratory coin marking ten years from one of my fellow sojourners. The bronze coin, marked by the

Roman numeral X in the middle, was circled by the words "One Day at a Time" and "To Thine Own Self Be True."

I held on to the coin for a minute and pressed into it all the gratitude I could muster before handing it over to my circle of fellows—my communion of desire. Each member held the coin for a few moments while they prayed silently for me. As I waited for the treasure to make its way around the sacred circle, my mind drifted back to that terrible, beautiful day when I was pulled over to the side of the road by the police to be ticketed for a DUI.

A terrible, beautiful wreck. Fear. Humiliation. Dread. Self-hatred. Tears dripped from my face as I remembered the ruins. Strangely, I thought about the shortest verse in the Bible: "Jesus wept" (John 11:35). I have come to believe that he weeps not about the wreckage of our lives but about everything we cannot know without understanding our story of grace—our genesis story. From the beginning, failure allows us to fall *into* Grace.

My mess has become my message: *There's hope in every moment, every conversation, every person we encounter.* Disappointment reorients our view of ourselves so that we are no longer the most important character in our story. Our failures are not the point. Our wrecks are not the point. We are not the point. In fact, wrecks are a relief, revealing we cannot save ourselves. We need a Savior.

As the ten-year coin that took me thirty years to find made its way back to me, I thought about the hundreds of faces who deserved to be imprinted into its bronze. Faces filled with sorrow, anger, confusion, hope, and grace. I recalled so many words I've heard along the path of recovery—words from my sponsor, my children, my parents, my pastor, my friends, my enemies, as well as tender words from Jesus during many dark nights of the soul, inviting me into grace. The many characters and conversations in my story of recovery still leave room for me—a sixty-year-old woman with a tattered, raggedy heart threaded with breathtaking, brilliantly colored ribbons of grace.

Unexpected grace whispers words I would have never believed while I sat in handcuffs in the back of a police car:

You're blessed in the very moment you're at the end of your rope.[1]

His Story swallows your story until, together, they become the deepest story.

Every Loss

One of the people witnessing my burning bush of ten years of sobriety was my daughter. She held the symbolic coin a little longer than the rest of the group. Our eyes met as our hearts collided in our story of love born and love gasping for its last breath, of our very lives being turned right side up while being turned upside down in moments we might have pushed aside, hurried through, or wished forgotten.

All those moments flashed before me. Every one. Moments of . . .

- Emotional devastation—this isn't the story I picked.
- Psychological chaos—this isn't a story that makes sense.
- Spiritual impoverishment—this isn't a story I believe.
- Cultural oppression—this is a story with scary characters, messy characters. They aren't winners.

Every one of those moments confirmed Jesus was writing a story designed for and specifically targeted at . . . *losers*.

Kristin passed my ten-year coin to the next person in the circle, got up out of her chair, walked straight to me, and whispered words we have said back and forth and back and forth and back and forth to each other for years. Words from an ancient script, written in a galaxy far away and long ago, outlining the battle plan for winning our hearts: "Nothing you can do can ever make me stop loving you."

Unexpected grace confirms the oh-too-good-to-be-true news, often announced in the worst possible moments:

You're blessed in the very moment when you feel you've lost what is most dear to you.

Only then can you be embraced by the One most dear to you.[2]

Only then does his story take up flesh and blood in your story. It becomes incarnate, and so do you—making Jesus Christ visible to all.

Every Person

I left the sacred celebration to return to the necessary daily tasks. My first client for the day was sixteen years old. Her year has been one of bone-aching loneliness as she's tried to find her place among her peers, hang on to her values, and not seem too weird. Her high-school résumé lacked a lot of the achievements the adolescent world requires (and maybe it's not just the adolescent world). She isn't popular. She doesn't wear trendy fashions. She's never been asked on a date. She doesn't even have Snapchat on her phone. Her reputation is as "a Goody Two-shoes" only the teachers like. She cried every time she told me about her incredibly painful high-school story and asked how she could change it. I encouraged her to be true to who God made her to be, and yet I knew those are words adults say when we don't really know what to say.

Her visit to see me on this day was right after the second semester of the school year started. She walked into my office with joy and confidence. If I didn't know better, I would think she was voted prom queen. I suspected she was just relieved to be halfway out of the hell of high school. I was wrong.

Danielle explained to me that she'd decided to do something with all her grief and pain over being unfairly judged and excluded. She wrote a letter to many of her classmates before the Christmas break, telling them what they meant to her and how she would be praying for them over the break. Part of me wanted to applaud her endeavor and another part wanted to shout, "No! You're just going to make yourself more of a target. Maybe you should be less of yourself and not more." (I knew that didn't sound very wise or counselor-like, so I just silently waited to hear the rest of the story.)

Danielle told me about one letter she wrote to a girl who came out as gay to her classmates the first semester. Her announcement resulted in a lot of teasing, and her parents kicked her out of their home. Danielle explained that she congratulated this girl on her courage—and especially for telling her when she knew Danielle didn't agree with her values about sexuality.

"I thanked her for telling me, even though she knows I'm a Christian, and I wanted her to know that I want to love her and support her. I don't want her to think God hates her, because I think God especially loves those of us who are the 'unfortunate ones' in high school. I told her I asked my parents, and they agreed she could stay with us if she ever needed a place to stay."

Tears welled in my eyes as my respect for this young woman grew. She sat up a little straighter and pulled a piece of paper out of her pocket. She gingerly handed it to me—conveying its inestimable value. Truly, it had been bought with a great price.

I read the note, scrawled in blue ink, blotted in places with what I suspect were tearstains.

Danielle, no one has ever written me an actual letter before!!! Your letter is the best thing that happened to me this year. I also want you to know I don't hate God and I don't think he hates me. Because of you. I might not stay at your house, but I definitely want to eat at your table in the cafeteria!!!!

In that very moment, I knew how Jesus would answer if anyone asked who was greatest in high school: "Truly I tell you, unless you change and become like little children, you will never enter the kingdom of heaven. Therefore, whoever takes the lowly position of this child is the greatest in the kingdom of heaven"(Matthew 18:3-4, NIV). For a little child, everything comes by grace, and they have no résumé. "Become like one of them!" says Jesus.

Danielle's incarnational love could silence all the trolls on social media and heal the cancer of fragmentation. She astounded me with the living reminder that God writes our true résumé, and he will reveal it in every moment, every conversation, every interaction. And the day will come when he will read our résumés—which will actually be our stories. I long for mine to sound something like this:

- "You gave me a cup of cold water."
- "I was hungry, and you shared your lunch."
- "I was the stranger, the loner at your school; you came and sat with me."

Unexpected grace invites us to let God write our résumés:

You're blessed the very moment when you're content
with just who you are—no more, no less. That's
the moment you find yourselves proud owners of
everything that can't be bought,[3] and everyone—
the liars, addicts, fools, and totally uncool—feels
welcome at your table.

Every Conflict

I don't remember the news on that day of my ten-year anniversary of sobriety. I'm sure it was bad. The next political
battle is just gearing up. Twitter is alive with the sounds
of hate, attack, blame, and self-rightness. It's easy to lose a
meaningful moment, like the one I had at my twelve-step
group or with Danielle, because this world is so much with
us. This world's division metastasizes into every nook and
cranny of our lives—our small group at church, our kids'
soccer team, book club, social media, family reunions.

The very same day with the highlights of my ten-year coin
and amazing hour with Danielle, I experienced lowlights in
line at the grocery store. It is hard not to look at the tabloids
and all the gossip and vitriol they shout from their place in
the racks right by the cash register. One man looked at a
picture of a newly elected female congresswoman and right
there—in the midst of Doritos and Raisin Bran and fiber
gummies (there's a story in there somewhere!)—he started a

rant about her I could never repeat. It was vile and mean, and I left with my bags full of groceries but very little appetite.

Perhaps you know what I'm talking about. You've read this book about discovering the deeper story, looking for grace in every person and every conversation, changing your own heart and your words and stretching your world to invite others to that same story. It *feels* transformative. And then real life hits us right in the gut while we're waiting to buy groceries. How can we experience transformation when the undertow of everything around us pulls us back into the muck of division? A recent survey confirmed that eight out of ten people feel we are completely, hopelessly divided from one another.[4]

The forest of debate, judgment, and condemnation can suffocate our longing for *More*. Canadian author Charles de Lint describes our plight: "We end up stumbling our way through the forest, never seeing all the unexpected and wonderful possibilities and potentials because we're looking for the idea of a tree, instead of appreciating the actual trees in front of us."[5] The only way to nurture a hunger for truth, beauty, and goodness is to stop looking at the forest of our culture. Unexpected grace sends us looking for trees.

Activist, writer, and poet Wendell Berry suggests a different approach to life than keeping our noses to our devices, our hearts in some political tumult, and our lives entrenched in the death of division:

> So, friends, every day do something
> that won't compute. . . .

Give your approval to all you cannot
understand. . . .
Ask the questions that have no answers. . . .
Put your faith in the two inches of humus
that will build under the trees
every thousand years. . . .
. . . Laugh.
Laughter is immeasurable. Be joyful
though you have considered all the facts. . . .
Practice resurrection.[6]

What does it mean for us to "practice resurrection?" It is living in the unexpected grace—the way of finding one another—by

- letting our need to be right die;
- killing our prejudice by being a place of refuge to others;
- caring about more than ourselves;
- pushing past apathy to kindness;
- looking for the invisible, those on the edges of our stories;
- speaking words of life, hope, and inclusion;
- laughing at ourselves;
- feeling deeply about ordinary people in ordinary moments;

- having faith in the goodness of people, and always—
  even when people let us down—having faith in the
  goodness of God; and
- acting as if we belong to one another so whatever
  we're in the middle of right now can be filled with
  redemptive truth, beauty, and goodness from the
  power of *withness*.

Practicing resurrection means cultivating our appetite for
More than this paltry, divided, flimsy world can offer and getting
busy living for *More*. Unexpected grace keeps us hungry:

> You're blessed at the very moment when you've
> worked up a good appetite for God.
> His story is the best food and drink in the best
> meal you'll ever eat or share with others.[7]

Every Care

I fell into bed the night of my tenth anniversary of sobriety
overwhelmed by all the ways God has shown his grace to
me—a self-centered, stumbling, bumbling woman who has
cared way too much about what others think, about alcohol,
about climbing up the ladder of achievement, about arriving
in the inner circle.

But God.

God has used failure, difficult people, my children,

heartache, falling down, getting back up, and falling down again to change what I care about. The paradox is that the more I stop making life all about me—my rights, hurts, demands, and judgments—the more I feel cared for by God. When we own our narcissistic tendencies (we all have them!), humble ourselves, really listen, stretch our comfort zone, freely give, don't hold back, and stop worrying about whether we are enough or there will be enough, we experience the unexpected grace of "every good and perfect gift . . . coming down from the Father of the heavenly lights" (James 1:17, NIV).

Only when we stop making our beleaguered, harried hearts central in our lives can our beleaguered, harried hearts rest in a care we cannot bestow on ourselves. I cannot help but smile when I read this definition of the freedom of surrendering what I care about to the care of God:

> All great spirituality teaches about letting go of
> what you don't need and who you are not. Then,
> when you can get little enough and naked enough
> and poor enough, you'll find that the little place
> where you really are is ironically more than enough
> and is all that you need. At that place, you will
> have nothing to prove to anybody and nothing
> to protect. That place is called freedom. It's the
> freedom of the children of God. Such people can
> connect with everybody. They don't feel the need to
> eliminate anybody.[8]

Unexpected grace envelops us in care:

You're blessed . . . in the very moment of being "care-full," because you will find yourself smack-dab in the middle of a story about being cared for.[9]

Every Story

Are you waiting to be surprised by Grace? It's easy to become cynical and bitter in this day—focusing on *them* and how *they* are stuck—and not participate in common grace or being transformed by grace. And then we miss the surprise of Grace. Here's a good question to prompt the next chapter in your story. Would you rather be alive and free and thrilled with all God is doing in your heart . . . or see *them* change? I am learning that there are the stories of the day and then there are the stories of eternity. Stories with any worth change our lives forever—perhaps only in a small way, but once we've heard them, they are forever a part of us, and then we nurture them and pass them on to one another.

As I drifted off to sleep after my day filled with celebration and reminders of defeat; with examples of love and hints of the hate still out there; with images of beautiful, fragrant green trees and visions of diseased forests; with strains of peaceful lullabies playing in my heart and the rumbles of war still in the distance, God whispered these unexpected words of grace: "Stop trying to write your own story! Let me keep writing, wait, and see."

Here's another way to put it: You're here to be light, bringing out the God-colors in the world. God is not a secret to be kept. We're going public with this, as public as a city on a hill. If I make you light-bearers, you don't think I'm going to hide you under a bucket, do you? I'm putting you on a light stand. Now that I've put you there on a hilltop, on a light stand— shine! Keep open house; be generous with your lives. By opening up to others, you'll prompt people to open up with God, this generous Father in heaven.
MATTHEW 5:14-16

With a little faith and hope in the story God is writing in *us*, we just might be on the way back to finding love and *belonging to one another*.

(into action)

1. Has there been a time when you were at the end of your rope, you let go, and you found yourself embraced by belovedness?

2. Find a moment to celebrate today. Share that moment with a few friends and ask to hear about their moments.

3. Is there someone you can invite today to be a part of your life? Have coffee? Play racquetball? Eat at your table?

4. Was there a moment of tension, conflict, division today? How did you handle it? How do you wish you'd handled it?

5. What are your cares and worries today? Maybe it's time to find another piece of glass, break it, and begin looking for God to form the mosaic of your story.

Courage, dear heart.

C. S. LEWIS[10]

Acknowledgments

Don Pape, publisher and friend extraordinaire. Thank you for knowing when this book was in me and always cheering me on.

Caitlyn Carlson, editor. Your thoughtful and wise insights made this a better book.

Elizabeth Schroll, copy editor. Your careful reading and research is invaluable.

Peter Hiett, my pastor. Although we no longer see each other often, you continue to relentlessly encourage me to believe the gospel. Thank you for the gift of your sermons.

Dan Allender, teacher and friend. Your words are on every page.

Rachel Canella, friend and advisor on word choice, stories, suffering, and great food, when sustenance is needed!

Susie Sellers, I am indebted to you for allowing me to hold and tell part of Kyle's story.

William and Dana Brereton. As Ralph Waldo Emerson wrote, "It is a luxury to be understood."[1]

Sharla Jackson Jepkes. Your vibrant love of others shows me the way back.

Danielle Stormer, you remind me that teenagers are people too.

Friends and clients: Thank you for joining me in a communion of stories.

John and Kathleen Baker, my parents, for the lifelong gift of belonging.

Graham Hersh, my son. Your love for songs and stories inspires me.

Kristin Hersh, my daughter. There are no words adequate enough to say thank you for the astounding privilege of telling your story and being a part of your still-unfolding story.

Notes

CHAPTER 1: THE WAY BACK

1. This opening story is revised from previous blog post "The Anatomy of Addiction (Rooted 2017 Workshop Preview)," *Rooted Ministry*, October 16, 2017, https://www.rootedministry.com/blog/anatomy-addiction-rooted-2017-workshop-preview/.
2. Samuel Johnson, *The Works of Samuel Johnson*, vol. 10 (Troy, NY: Pafraets Book Company, 1903), 267.
3. Robert Benson, *Between the Dreaming and the Coming True: The Road Home to God* (New York: Tarcher/Putnam, 2001), 9.
4. John D. Blasé, editor, Facebook post, May 19, 2016.
5. Chuck DeGroat, *Falling into Goodness: Lenten Reflections* (CreateSpace, 2017), 4. Used with permission.

CHAPTER 2: THE PRELUDE: APPETITES

1. Tim Minchin, "Quiet," *Matilda the Musical*, Royal Shakespeare Company, 2010.
2. Pete Seeger, "We Shall Overcome," *We Shall Overcome: Complete Carnegie Hall Concert* © 1989 Sony Legacy. This song became "the anthem of the civil-rights movement," and, eventually, "the marching song in battles for freedom around the world," Allan M. Winkler, "We Shall Overcome," *American Heritage* 62, no. 5 (fall 2017), https://www.americanheritage.com/we-shall-overcome.
3. Philip Yancey, *What's So Amazing about Grace?* (Grand Rapids, MI: Zondervan, 2002), 99.
4. Oliver Sacks, "Altered States," *The New Yorker*, August 20, 2012, https://www.newyorker.com/magazine/2012/08/27/altered-states-3.

5. Vocabulary.com, s.v. "transcendence," accessed November 7, 2019, https://www.vocabulary.com/dictionary/transcendence.

6. Parker J. Palmer, *The Politics of the Brokenhearted: On Holding the Tensions of Democracy* (Kalamazoo, MI: Fetzer Institute, 2005), 232.

7. Palmer, *Politics of the Brokenhearted*, 232.

8. Caroline Knapp, *Appetites: Why Women Want* (New York: Counterpoint, 2004), 45.

9. Aric Jenkins, "Study Finds That Half of Americans—Especially Young People—Feel Lonely," Fortune.com, May 1, 2018, https://fortune.com /2018/05/01/americans-lonely-cigna-study/.

10. C. S. Lewis, *The Weight of Glory: and Other Addresses* (New York: HarperOne, 2001), 26: "It would seem that Our Lord finds our desires not too strong, but too weak."

11. Palmer, *Politics of the Brokenhearted*, 244.

12. Palmer, *Politics of the Brokenhearted*, 245.

13. Quoted in Jack Canfield and Mark Victor Hansen, *A 3rd Serving of Chicken Soup for the Soul: More Stories to Open the Heart and Rekindle the Spirit* (Cos Cob, CT: Backlist, 2012), introduction.

14. Peter Hiett, "The Tree in the Middle of the Garden," Denver: The Sanctuary, January 20, 2019, https://relentless-love.org/wp-content/ uploads/2019/01/20190120-43 -The-Tree-in-the-Middle-of-the-Garden.pdf. Peter brilliantly guides us to think about some of the stories I mention and more.

15. Andy Gullahorn, "Why You Brought Me Here," *The Law of Gravity*, 2009. Used with permission. You can listen to it at https://www.youtube.com /watch?v=PFCG00ee1CU.

CHAPTER 3: THE CAST OF CHARACTERS

1. Andrew Peterson, "The Silence of God," *Love and Thunder* © Essential Records, 2003.

2. Parker J. Palmer, *A Hidden Wholeness: The Journey toward an Undivided Life* (San Francisco, CA: Jossey-Bass, 2009), 38–39.

3. *The Big Book of Alcoholics Anonymous*, 4th ed. (New York: Alcoholics Anonymous World Services, 2001), 62.

4. Palmer, *Hidden Wholeness*, 38–39.

5. M. Scott Peck, *People of the Lie: The Hope for Healing Human Evil* (New York: Touchstone, 1983), 105.

6. Peter Hiett, "Not So Good to Be King" (or "Why God Is So Uptight about Sin"), Denver: The Sanctuary, August 18, 2014, https://relentless-love.org /sermons/not-so-good-to-be-king-or-why-god-is-so-uptight-about-sin/.

7. Peterson, "The Silence of God."
8. Max Lucado, "God as Heart Surgeon (EXCERPT)," *Huffington Post*, updated November 19, 2012, https://www.huffpost.com /entry/god-as-heart-surgeon_b_1874927.
9. Ann Voskamp, *The Way of Abundance: A 60-Day Journey into a Deeply Meaningful Life* (Grand Rapids, MI: Zondervan, 2018), devotion 28.

CHAPTER 4: THE TWIST IN THE PLOT
1. Sarah Cunningham, ed., *Inciting Incidents: 6 Stories of Fighting Disappointment in a Flawed World* (Chicago, IL: Moody Publishers, 2012), afterword.
2. Zora Neale Hurston, *Dust Tracks on a Road: An Autobiography* (New York: HarperPerennial, 1996), 176.
3. Dan Allender, "Understanding Your Story," *And Sons Magazine* no. 7 (October 2014), https://archive.andsonsmagazine.com/07/understanding -your-story-interview-dan-allender#.XcnV-jNKhjU.
4. Henri Nouwen, *Life of the Beloved: Spiritual Living in a Secular World* (New York: Crossroad, 2002), 33.
5. Allender, "Understanding Your Story."
6. Bob Goff, Facebook post, September 27, 2019.
7. Revelation 3:20.
8. W. H. Auden, *The Age of Anxiety: A Baroque Eclogue* (Princeton, NJ: Princeton University Press, 2011), 105.
9. Richard J. Foster, *Prayer: Finding the Heart's True Home* (HarperSanFrancisco, 1998), 1.
10. Richard Rohr, "The Meaning of Spiritual Love," Center for Action and Contemplation, November 7, 2018, https://cac.org/the-meaning -of-spiritual-love-2018-11-07/.
11. Allender, "Understanding Your Story."
12. "How to Step into God's Story," *Relevant* magazine, September 11, 2012, https://relevantmagazine.com/god/how-step-gods-story/.
13. Sarah Hepola, "Anne Lamott: 'We stuffed scary feelings down, and they made us insane,'" Salon.com, November 4, 2014, https://www.salon .com/2014/11/04/anne_lamott_we_stuffed_scary_feelings_down_and _they_made_us_insane/.

CHAPTER 5: THE POSTLUDE: LITTLE EARTHQUAKES EVERYWHERE
1. Kristin Hersh, "It started in college," Facebook post, July 2018.
2. Tori Amos, "Little Earthquakes," *Little Earthquakes* © 1992 Atlantic Records.

3. Rainer Maria Rilke, *Letters to a Young Poet* (New York: W. W. Norton, 1993), 41.

4. Rilke, *Letters*, 41.

5. Louisa M. R. Stead, "'Tis So Sweet to Trust in Jesus," 1882.

6. James Clay Corrigan, "I know that many people will watch," Facebook post, October 4, 2016.

7. Margery Williams, *The Velveteen Rabbit* (New York: Doubleday, 1997), 7.

8. Quoted by the School of Practical Philosophy, https://practicalphilosophy. org.au/discard-yourself-and-thereby-regain-yourself-spread-the-trap-of -humility-and-ensnare-love-rumi/.

9. "The Story You Fell Into," Ransomed Heart, accessed November 12, 2019, https://www.ransomedheart.com/story/larger-story/story-you-fell-into.

10. Mother Teresa, *Where There Is Love, There Is God: A Path to Closer Union with God and Greater Love for Others* (New York: Doubleday, 2010), 330.

11. Jennifer Weiner, *Little Earthquakes* (New York: Washington Square Press, 2005), 5.

12. Bob Goff, *Everybody, Always: Becoming Love in a World Full of Setbacks and Difficult People* (Nashville: Thomas Nelson, 2018), 168.

13. Quoted by Neal Klein, "A Poem by Gwen Flowers Entitled Grief," *Life After Emilee* (blog), December 30, 2017, https://www.lifeafteremilee .com/a-poem-by-gwen-flowers-entitled-grief/.

CHAPTER 6: CHANGING YOU IN THE STORY

1. Brian A. Primack et al., "The Association between Valence of Social Media Experience and Depressive Symptoms," *Depression and Anxiety* 35, no. 8 (August 2018): 787.

2. Barna Group, "The State of the Church 2016," September 15, 2016, accessed November 14, 2019, https://www.barna.com/research /state-church-2016/.

3. Anissa Lotti, "Why People Really Don't Like Christians," Crosswalk.com, June 8, 2016, https://www.crosswalk.com/faith/spiritual-life/why-people -really-don-t-like-christians.html.

4. Jessie Klein, "Girls Get Called 'Slut' Everyday," *Psychology Today*, March 8, 2012, https://www.psychologytoday.com/us/blog/creating -compassionate-communities/201203/girls-get-called-slut-everyday.

5. "Teen Trend Report: Where Has Civility Gone?" StageofLife.com, accessed November 14, 2019, https://www.stageoflife.com/StageHighSchool /TeensandCivility.aspx.

6. Bill Hendrick, "Internet Addiction Spins Web of Depression," WebMD.com,

February 4, 2010, https://www.webmd.com/depression/news/20100204
/internet-addiction-linked-to-depression#1.

7. "Social Anxiety Disorder," Anxiety and Depression Association of America,
accessed November 14, 2019, https://adaa.org/understanding
-anxiety/social-anxiety-disorder.

8. David Niose, "Beware America's Shocking Loss of Empathy: The
Symptoms of a Society Coming Unhinged," *Psychology Today*, March 6,
2016, https://www.psychologytoday.com/us/blog/our-humanity
-naturally/201603/beware-americas-shocking-loss-empathy.

9. Brynn Tannehill, "Here's the Reason Why Fewer Americans Are Christian
That Evangelicals Don't Want You to Know," *LGBTQ Nation*, June 10,
2018, https://www.lgbtqnation.com/2018/06/heres-reason-fewer
-americans-christian-evangelicals-dont-want-know/.

10. John Pavlovitz, "Maybe I'm Actually Not a Christian After All," *Stuff That
Needs to Be Said* (blog), January 27, 2016, https://johnpavlovitz
.com/2016/01/27/maybe-im-actually-not-a-christian-after-all/.

11. Quoted in Daisy Luther, "We're Being Programmed by Social Media," *The
Real Agenda News*, May 17, 2018, https://real-agenda.com/world-3
/we-are-being-programmed-social-media/.

12. Carolyn Gregoire, "Why Loneliness Is a Growing Public Health
Concern—and What We Can Do about It," *HuffPost*, March 21, 2015,
https://www.huffpost.com/entry/science-loneliness_n_6864066.

13. Diane Kalen-Sukra, *Save Your City: How Toxic Culture Kills Community &
What to Do About It* (Victoria, BC: TellWell Talent, 2019), 46.

14. Donald Miller, quoted in Dennis Okholm, *Monk Habits for Everyday
People: Benedictine Spirituality for Protestants* (Grand Rapids, MI: Brazos
Press, 2007), 73–74.

15. Okholm, *Monk Habits*, 75.

16. Don Hazen, "Fear Dominates Politics, Media, and Human Existence in
America—And It's Getting Worse," AlterNet.org, March 1, 2015, https://
www.alternet.org/2015/03/fear-dominates-politics-media-and-human
-existence-america-and-its-getting-worse/.

17. Baltasar Gracián, *The Art of Worldly Wisdom* (Overland Park, KS:
Digireads, 2018), 39.

18. Timothy Keller, "What Is Common Grace?" AndyandJanine.com,
September 26, 2017, http://andyandjanine.com/what-is-common
-grace-tim-keller/.

19. William P. Young, *The Shack : A Novel* (Newbury Park, CA: Windblown
Media, 2007), 92.

20. Young, *The Shack*, 95.

21. Young, *The Shack*, 96.
22. Young, *The Shack*, 136.
23. Young, *The Shack*, 207.
24. Phil Vaughn, "What if the problem isn't really the issue?" Facebook post, April 29, 2019.
25. Young, *The Shack*, 181.
26. Young, *The Shack*, 187.
27. Vaughn, "What if the problem isn't really the issue?"

CHAPTER 7: CHANGING THE CONVERSATION

1. As cited in Conor Lynch, "America May Be More Divided Now than at Any Time Since the Civil War," Salon.com, October 14, 2017, https://www.Salon.com/2017/10/14/america-may-be-more-divided-now-than-at-any-time
-since-the-civil-war/.
2. Dietrich Bonhoeffer, *The Cost of Discipleship* (New York: Touchstone, 1995), 185.
3. Rachel Held Evans, *Searching for Sunday: Loving, Leaving, and Finding the Church* (Nashville: Thomas Nelson, 2015), 73.
4. Evans, *Searching for Sunday*, xvi.
5. *The Collected Letters of C. S. Lewis, Vol. III, 1950–1963*, ed. Walter Hooper (HarperSanFrancisco, 2007), 111; C. S. Lewis, *God in the Dock* (Grand Rapids, MI: Eerdmans, 1970), 310.
6. These thoughts about theology came from a sermon by Peter Hiett, "Offended? (You Don't Vote for King)," Denver: The Sanctuary, May 23, 2004, https://relentless-love.org/sermons/offended-you-dont-vote
-for-king/.
7. For more on "the curse of Cain," see http://www.bibleodyssey.net/people/related-articles/mark-of-cain.aspx.
8. Donald Miller, *Scary Close: Dropping the Act and Finding True Intimacy* (Nashville: Thomas Nelson, 2014), 97–98.
9. Brené Brown, *Men, Women, and Worthiness: The Experience of Shame and the Power of Being Enough* (Sounds True, 2012), audible.com.
10. Robert Capon, "The Message of Jesus: Interview with Robert F. Capon," interview by Tim Brassell, Grace Communion International, 2004, https://www.gci.org/articles/interview-with-robert-f-capon/.
11. Anna McCarthy, "'I Was Shocked by What I Saw': The Night I Went Strip Clubbing with Pastors' Wives," FaithIt.com, May 22, 2018, https://faithit.com/night-went-strip-clubbing-pastors-wives/.
12. Quoted in Rachel Held Evans, *Inspired: Slaying Giants, Walking on Water, and Loving the Bible Again* (Nashville, TN: Thomas Nelson, 2018), 186.

13. Kristin Hersh, Facebook post, February 2017.
14. Evans, *Searching for Sunday*, 148.
15. Evans, *Searching for Sunday*, 149.
16. Bob Goff, *Love Does: Discover a Secretly Incredible Life in an Ordinary World* (Nashville, TN: Thomas Nelson, 2012), 8–9.

CHAPTER 8: CHANGING THE CAST OF CHARACTERS
1. Lexico, s.v. "marginalization (*n.*)," accessed December 4, 2019, https://www.lexico.com/en/definition/marginalization.
2. Marcia Kester Doyle, "The Invisible Generation," *HuffPost*, March 25, 2015, https://www.huffpost.com/entry/the-invisible-generation_b_6938344.
3. *Oxford English Dictionary*, s.v. "prejudice."
4. Mark Labberton, *The Dangerous Act of Loving Your Neighbor: Seeing Others through the Eyes of Jesus* (Downers Grove, IL: InterVarsity Press, 2010), 180.
5. David Brooks, *The Second Mountain: The Quest for a Moral Life* (New York: Random House, 2019), 62.
6. Cory Collins, "What is White Privilege, Really?" *Teaching Tolerance* 60 (fall 2018), https://www.tolerance.org/magazine/fall-2018/what-is-white-privilege-really.
7. Walter Brueggemann, *Awed to Heaven, Rooted in Earth: Prayers of Walter Brueggemann* (Minneapolis, MN: Fortress Press, 2002), 76.
8. Brooks, *Second Mountain*, xii.
9. Jim Wallis, "Why?" *Sojourners on the Issues*, www.Sojo.net, March–April 1998.
10. Labberton, *Dangerous Act*, 170.
11. Stanley J. Grenz, *Sexual Ethics: An Evangelical Perspective* (Louisville, KY: Westminster John Knox Press, 1993), 197.
12. Wendell Berry, *Sex, Economy, Freedom & Community: Eight Essays* (New York: Pantheon Books, 1993), 120.
13. Michael Ford, *Wounded Prophet: A Portrait of Henri J. M. Nouwen* (New York: Image Books, 2002), 142.
14. Ronald Rolheiser, "The Vale of Tears," RonRolheiser.com, July 10, 1992, https://ronrolheiser.com/the-vale-of-tears/#.XdRe0FdKhjU.
15. Brooks, *Second Mountain*, xiii.

CHAPTER 9: EVERY MOMENT
1. Author's paraphrase of Matthew 5:3, MSG.
2. Author's paraphrase of Matthew 5:4, MSG.

3. Author's paraphrase of Matthew 5:5, MSG.

4. Dante Chinni and Sally Bronston, "Americans Are Divided over Everything Except Division," NBCNews.com, October 21, 2018, https://www.nbcnews.com/politics/first-read/americans-are-divided-over-everything-except-division-n922511.

5. Charles de Lint, *Tapping the Dream Tree* (New York: Tor, 2002), 291.

6. Wendell Berry, *The Country of Marriage: Poems* (Berkeley, CA: Counterpoint, 2013), 15–16.

7. Author's paraphrase of Matthew 5:6, MSG.

8. Richard Rohr, *Healing Our Violence through the Journey of Centering Prayer* (Albuquerque, NM: Centre for Action and Contemplation, 2013), CD.

9. Author's paraphrase of Matthew 5:7, MSG.

10. C. S. Lewis, *The Voyage of the* Dawn Treader (New York: HarperCollins, 1994), 203.

ACKNOWLEDGMENTS

1. Ralph Waldo Emerson, *Journals and Miscellaneous Notebooks: 1826–1832* (Cambridge, MA: Belknap Press, 1963), 244.

THE NAVIGATORS® STORY

T HANK YOU for picking up this NavPress book! I hope it has been a blessing to you.

NavPress is a ministry of The Navigators. The Navigators began in the 1930s, when a young California lumberyard worker named Dawson Trotman was impacted by basic discipleship principles and felt called to teach those principles to others. He saw this mission as an echo of 2 Timothy 2:2: "And the things you have heard me say in the presence of many witnesses entrust to reliable people who will also be qualified to teach others" (NIV).

In 1933, Trotman and his friends began discipling members of the US Navy. By the end of World War II, thousands of men on ships and bases around the world were learning the principles of spiritual multiplication by the intentional, person-to-person teaching of God's Word.

After World War II, The Navigators expanded its relational ministry to include college campuses; local churches; the Glen Eyrie Conference Center and Eagle Lake Camps in Colorado Springs, Colorado; and neighborhood and citywide initiatives across the country and around the world.

Today, with more than 2,600 US staff members—and local ministries in more than 100 countries—The Navigators continues the transformational process of making disciples who make more disciples, advancing the Kingdom of God in a world that desperately needs the hope and salvation of Jesus Christ and the encouragement to grow deeper in relationship with Him.

NAVPRESS was created in 1975 to advance the calling of The Navigators by bringing biblically rooted and culturally relevant products to people who want to know and love Christ more deeply. In January 2014, NavPress entered an alliance with Tyndale House Publishers to strengthen and better position our rich content for the future. Through *THE MESSAGE* Bible and other resources, NavPress seeks to bring positive spiritual movement to people's lives.

If you're interested in learning more or becoming involved with The Navigators, go to www.navigators.org. For more discipleship content from The Navigators and NavPress authors, visit www.thedisciplemaker.org. May God bless you in your walk with Him!

Sincerely,

DON PAPE
VP/PUBLISHER, NAVPRESS

www.navpress.com

CP1308